The Innocent Days of a North Dakota Farm Boy

Carmen James Lee

ISBN: 978-1-4834-3266-3 (sc)
ISBN: 978-1-4834-3267-0 (hc)
ISBN: 978-1-4834-3265-6 (e)

Library of Congress Control Number: 2015909171

Lulu Publishing Services rev. date: 6/11/2015

In memory of Mom and Dad, who were far from perfect but I loved them without reserve. Only after becoming an adult did I realize they were like most parents. They were not perfect.

In memory of Ronald (Lawrence or Red) and Janet who died much too young. Their lives, as much older siblings, made my childhood rich, fun and exciting. They left behind Glorine (Ronald) and John (Janet) who I treasure as family.

To Joan, Dave and Helen, my living siblings. Even though life took us hundreds of miles apart it seems our hearts have remained linked together. As we grow older our love becomes richer.

To grandchildren Henry, Liam, Leo, Faustina, Audrey, Jude, Ruby, Benedict, Agatha, Elspeth, Veronica and any more grandchildren who may come. Each generation brings new hope, new dreams and new adventures. Your generation will be one to be proud of. These stories are meant to provide entertainment and give you understanding about your roots.

Acknowledge

Thank you to Mom and Dad. Growing up money was scarce but we had a wonderful life, lacking nothing of importance. They guided me through my stuttering years with flying colors, relying only on parental love and wisdom. I am eternally grateful. I would not trade my childhood for anything.

Ronald and Janet were older siblings who were paramount in my childhood. I thought they walked on water and often prayed that they would come home to visit. Ronald died at the age of 28 and sixteen months later Janet died at the age of 27. As a nineteen year old college freshman, I was without my heroes and mentors. I still miss them and wonder what life would have been like if they had lived into old age.

Thank you to my living siblings, Joan, Dave and Helen. Many memories were created with you. Without the games, the activities and the work we did together, my childhood would have been normal or perhaps mundane and boring. As I wrote and sent you e-mails of my writing, your encouragement was tremendous. Your insights and correction of details that I missed were helpful.

My biggest thank you goes to my wife, Terry. Without your encouragement, your ideas, your editing and your love, these stories would only be memories. You put up with messes of paper and pictures that required much patience and forgiveness during the many months of compiling this book. On that cool blustery day in October, when you challenged me to write a 50,000 word book in the month, I said no. I knew I was not capable of tackling such a task, but you persisted. I will always be indebted to you.

Illustrations and Photos

All photos are family photos taken by my dad, Lawrence, who died in 1997. He was passionate about his photography. I am still reaping the benefits of his work.

Andy Grams sketched all the illustrations except the music. The sheet music was provided by my brother, Dave, one of the proud soldiers to Mom's march.

RL Caron edited the cover photo. He used an old photo, taken by my Dad, and edited it as only a professional could do. His advice and his knowledge of photos for book covers was greatly appreciated.

Prologue

It was a time of innocence. I grew up on a small farm in southeastern North Dakota. We were ten miles from our post office town and fifteen miles from a real town! Most of my time was spent with Mom, Dad and siblings Ronald, Janet, Joan, Dave and Helen. I was child number five in our family of six. Ronald was eleven years older and Helen is three years younger than I.

Most people would say I was born with Mom's temperament and I would agree. I was shy, withdrawn and reserved, perhaps fitting the stereo-type of a young boy with a speech impediment. For several years of my childhood I was a severe stutterer. I remember standing in front of the classroom in fifth grade and being unable to say a word. Time and God's healing made stuttering a distant memory by the time I was in high school.

"Carmen" may be embedded in the meaning of innocence. I barely knew how boys and girls were different. My understanding of the birds and the bees was blackbirds were good targets for my marksmanship and bees made honey! Mom's definition of sex was her story of Helen. As an adult she confided: *Your dad was deer hunting for a week. I missed him and knew he was coming home on Sunday. My sister Bertie did my hair and I put on my best dress. When your dad came in the front door he remarked how pretty I looked. Helen was born nine months later!* That paints a good picture of how much I knew as a child and how educated I was in "life".

I thought the worst swear words in the world were "What in the Sam Hill". That was as graphic as Dad got. Even though we had little money we always had enough to eat. I had no idea people were starving in the world. I did not think about people of a different color. I doubt I ever heard the word "prejudice". I thought every family had a mom and a dad who loved them. I envisioned the whole world to be like mine. My world where I could play in the mud after a rain, ride my bike to the lake, enjoy fried egg sandwiches for Sunday lunch, play make-believe and have a full tummy at bedtime.

Even in high school my innocence was evident. I went to my first high school dance as a freshman in the fall of 1961. I stood near the gym bleachers most of the night with all the other boys and watched. As the dance was coming to an end a girl came and asked me to dance. I was flustered because I had never danced in my life but I said "yes". She put her cheek on my shoulder and I did not understand why a shiver ran down my spine. When she asked if I would take her home I was surprised but said "yes" again. My entire freshman year I dated her and was amazed that anyone would be interested in me.

I did what many boys in high school do. I played sports, I dated and I didn't study as much as I should have. Through it all I am sure my innocence and naivety were stark.

The following stories are true stories of my childhood. In some stories there are details that are fuzzy in my mind but I wrote them to the best of my recollection. They are meant to give insights into a rural North Dakota upbringing. They do paint a picture of innocence and naivety that is perhaps lost in today's world. If it has been lost, please read and enjoy what was!

Index

Chapter One

I REMEMBER

I have always been a person who does not look back and wish my life had been different. I look ahead with a positive attitude and cheery outlook. However, I often enjoy sitting back with a cup of French press coffee in the morning or a cold brew in the afternoon and reflecting on those lazy, crazy, fun days of my childhood. Following is a collage of memories, some of which I will write about in the following chapters.

I remember the many dogs we had on the farm. Tiny was the best, Benny was the biggest, and Grandma Lee's Whitey was the blackest! The most disappointing was when our cocker spaniel disappeared. We never found her. The saddest was when our little puppy had to be put down. Dave and I were carrying a heavy pipe and one of us dropped it. Our new, tiny puppy, which followed us all the time, was pinned to the ground with a broken back.

I loved birthdays. One year Grandma Lee gave me a huge sugar cookie with a smiley face on it. It was the best. I have pictures of having more birthday cakes than I was years old. I don't know who ate them all. In sixth grade, my friend Larry stayed overnight for my birthday and Mom made fried spring chicken. Yum!

Mom's spring chicken is finger licking good
Dad, Mom, Carmen and Larry Fangsrud

I would often treat calves like babies. I would make a small pen in the yard and then play with them all day. Sometimes they seemed thirsty so I would let them suck on my toes. Then I would put a tiny rope around their necks and lead them around the yard. I pretended my calf was the grand show champion at the fair.

We made an adventure out of walking home from rural Wood Lake School in the winter. It took a long time because we kids would take turns running and jumping into the ditch to see who could land the deepest in the snow.

In late summer I would venture, with Grandma Lee, into the trees across the road from her house. There we would dig horse radish plants from among the trees. Grandma would grind it up and put it in jars. One time we sent a jar of horse radish to Aunt Ragna in California, as a thank you for the boxes of used clothes she sent. Not knowing what it was, she opened the jar and breathed in deeply. She said she almost passed out!

Picking choke cherries at Lake Tewaukon was a sour experience! The trees would be bent over with cherries. After hours of picking we would arrive home with gallon buckets full and faces stained purple. It was then only a short time before Mom would have fresh choke cherry syrup for cream and bread.

Mumps was a prolonged illness. I slept on the downstairs couch for many days. I looked like a pocket gopher during that time. Mom would make milk toast, and then when I felt better she would feed me a soft-boiled egg on toast.

Drowning gophers along the creek bank in the pasture was fun. We would have gallon pails to fetch water from the creek and pour down the hole. Finally, after many gallons of water, the drenched gophers would appear and we would chase them down with a stick. No more dangerous holes in our pasture!

The rock dam in the pasture, below the outhouse, was the source of much fun. During the spring flood, fish would get caught and we would be able to pick them up out of the rocks.

I could jump on my pogo stick from the house to the barn without falling off. I could even turn around and jump back to the house when I became very good!

We played ping-pong, in the winter, on our round kitchen table. After adding two leaves, we had an oval table that was a challenge to play on. Since there are no corners on an oval table, there were no corner shots practiced in our game!

We often had to shovel water out of the cattle pen, in the barn, after I left the water running in the tank too long.

Stacking hay, in the heat of the summer, provided adventure, fun and a lot of work. Occasionally while on top of the stack, I would step too close to the edge. Helplessly I would softly and safely slip and slide down the side and end up on the ground. I would then have to wave to Dad so he could drive the hay stacker over and give me a lift in the bucket up to the top again. I thought riding in the bucket was fun. I may even have slid down the side of the stack on purpose once or twice!

Running barefoot through the thistle patches during harvest was a fun thing to do. Look, *Mom, my feet are like leather*!

Many Sunday afternoons were spent in Bert's pasture shooting gophers. Dad would drive the car into the pasture and shut the engine off. We would then roll down the windows, stick the gun barrel out and whistle. When curiosity got the best of the gophers they stuck their heads up to see. Ka-boom!

One of our favorite games was kick-the-can. By the dim glow of the yard light, we would hide, run and have a grand time when cousins came to visit.

Our one-room school house always put on a Christmas program. My part, when I was in the third grade, was reciting the Christmas story from memory. Mom said she thought I would never get to the end.

It was special when we arrived home from school and there were saltine crackers with cake frosting on them sitting on a plate in the kitchen. We would hurry home if we thought that treat might be waiting for us.

There was the Little League baseball game in Cayuga. I struck out my first two times at bat. I came up in the last inning with our team two runs down, two outs and baserunners on second and third. I can still hear the sound of the bat as it connected with the ball. It soared over the right fielder's head as I rounded first and headed towards second base. When I crossed home plate, with the winning run, the ball was still in the outfielder's glove. Coach Murray said he knew I could do it! That cemented my idea that I had to wear this certain shirt. It was cream colored with three red stripes across the chest. I always felt like a great baseball player when I wore my lucky shirt!

In my egg picking days, I amazed Mom. One day I came back and in my bib-overall pockets there were eggs bulging out in every direction. Mom was concerned that I would break some but I gave her all thirteen, unharmed.

Sometimes, when we walked down into the pasture to get the cows for milking, we would stop by a huge rock on the creek bank. There would often be many snakes sunning themselves on the rock, thus the name Snake Rock came into to being!

I remember going from rural Wood Lake School to Cayuga School. Wood Lake was a one room school that had all eight grades and a total of twelve students in the spring of 1956. In the fall of that year I walked into my new classroom and there were twenty-four classmates staring at me. I was shocked.

In the late 50's, I decided to make a golf course. I created my very own, one-hole county club in our farm yard. I put the scoop on the back of the Ford tractor and got many loads of sand from the beaches of Lake Tewaukon. After five gallons of oil was mixed with the sand, I had my putting green, or should I say putting sand?

Picking weeds, for days, in the rows of trees we planted on the farm was far from my favorite work. Dad planted several groves of trees, in strategic places, to prevent snow from blocking our roads. He would cultivate between the rows and we had to pick the weeds between the tiny trees. It was a terrific science lesson with the brown, green and multi-colored worms in the weeds. I remember thinking I had never seen anything with so many legs.

Milking in the winter was an enjoyable experience. I would walk to the barn with the kerosene lantern in one hand and the milk pails in the other. When I entered the barn, the aroma and warmth from the cows would bid me welcome. After putting kickers on the cow, the first squirt of milk would hit the pail and beady eyes would appear in the darkness. After the cats were satisfied, I would settle onto the one legged stool and finish milking. I hated to venture out into the cold again after experiencing the warmth of the barn. Mom would be waiting to pour the milk into the cream separator, which was tucked into the corner of our entryway, when I walked back into the house. As the milk swirled around in the huge stainless steel tub, cream would come out on the right and milk would come out on the left.

Dad's stern demeanor and swift discipline were never far from my mind. The other side of the equation was Mom's gentle spirit and loving care. Both were usually dished out in ample amounts and with good timing.

Mom and Dad outside our farm house

I cringed every time Mom spit in her hand and tried to tame my hair with her damp hand. I also hated it when she insisted I put my earlaps down before I ventured out into the cold. The earlaps would usually go up as soon as Mom was out of sight. Many people would call them earflaps but to us they were earlaps.

We begged Mom to sit at the piano and play her marching song. When she started, we would get in a line and march in a figure eight through the living room, into the kitchen and then back again. The louder she played, the higher we lifted our legs and the more our heads pitched backward!

I was so proud when my brother Ronald gave me my first rifle, a 22. It was mine, it was from my idol and I have it to this day.

Wood Lake School, the memories are many and the stories are fun to tell.

The "Tractor Taxi" story is one for the ages. Would anyone, today, drive 10 miles in a snowstorm to get their son to school?

I remember the excitement when we prepared for deer hunting in the North Dakota Badlands. For several days I got to live with the men and be one of them. I thought it was "big time" when we would stop for lunch in the field. I would take out my hunting knife, cut a huge slice of sausage and enjoy. We never made sandwiches as that wasn't the "hunting way"! Sometimes I would sharpen my hunting knife until the blade looked like it wanted to give up! Perhaps I overdid it but it sure worked great for gutting a deer and slicing the sausage.

As I gathered fireflies near the bridge on the east end of Lake Tewaukon, I thought God sent them as a sign that the world is beautiful.

I loved to grind the deer meat for burgers and then watch Mom wrap and freeze it. That was the only time that the number of burgers I was allowed to eat was unlimited.

I remember carrying 5 gallon cans of kerosene into the house and pouring it into the back of the stove in the living room. If I spilled, the unpleasant smell of kerosene would hang in the house for hours.

Some winter nights, I went to sleep with the light on in my bedroom counting the frost covered nail heads in the ceiling. As I counted, I would blow my breath into the air and watch the lazy cloud of vapor disappear into the night.

One evening Joan, Dave and I were home alone. Late in the night, we saw car lights coming up the road and then slow to a crawl as they approached our farm. We hid, with fear in our hearts that the car would turn in and we would be robbed. We thought about Dad's guns upstairs but decided, no. When it slowly motored out of sight to the north, together we breathed a huge sigh of relief.

Joan would wash the dishes while Dave and I dried them. It was not our favorite task. Water had to be heated on the stove and then dishes were washed and dried in pans on the kitchen table. Joan said there were different points for different dishes as we dried them. She would never tell us our point total until all the dishes were dry. We always tied and I wondered why?

I thought the entire world revolved around sports. I thought Harry Caray was next to God and the St. Louis Cardinals were the best team in the world. I ordered a St Louis Cardinal baseball pen and when it came, I slept with it.

There was nothing more important than baseball cards. The Milwaukee Braves were my heroes when they beat the Yankees in 1957.

I was ecstatic when I was old enough to put those darn bib overalls away for good. Dad did not wear them and I felt I should not have to either. From early grade school, it was jeans with a real belt!

I remember these and many more adventures as I savor my French press coffees or my cold brews; life was good. As you read about these memories and more, please stop for a moment and remember the blessings in your life as well. Sit back, relax, remember and enjoy.

Chapter Two

GAMES WE PLAYED

I would like everyone to believe we worked all the time but of course that would be far from the truth. Did we work? We actually worked six days a week most of the time. Dave and I did much of the field work and I know my sisters helped Mom all the time in the house. However, we played a lot too. I played with Ricky, who lived a half mile north of us on a farm on the lake shore. Often we played with cousins and there were always games at Farmers Union meetings. Cousins and Farmers Union aside, most of our play was at home with siblings. Games were usually played with siblings Helen, Dave and Joan. Ronald and Janet were much older, so by the time I could play games they were boarding in Lidgerwood where they went to high school.

We had no electronic games in the fifties and sixties. We had board games, puzzles, cards, ping pong paddles, Lincoln Logs, and erector sets to occupy our time. Kernels of corn, old rifle cartridges, pieces of scrap wood and more came into play with our "made up games". In today's world a person may separate what we did into "games" and "activities". In our world, when we worked on the farm most of the time, everything that took up our time in a fun way was a game.

On rainy days our energy would almost implode the house so Mom, for sanity sake, came up with a game that we loved and took us many QUIET hours. We had this huge slate blackboard that measured four feet by three feet. About the time our energy reached its peak, instead of yelling at us Mom would drag out the slate and we knew we were in for a fun time. She would lay it on the living room floor and ask us what we wanted her to draw. With chalk in hand she would kneel down and do art work on the slate. When she finished our task was to take kernels of corn, which we kept in an old bucket, and cover all the chalk lines. Of course she would make the drawing rather complicated so it would take us a long time to cover the lines. It was an excellent way to exercise "crowd control". It also gave Mom her kitchen, as we would often beg to use the round table for ping pong.

Dave and I would spend hours and hours playing with empty shell casings from Dad's reloading hobby. Dad mostly reloaded 30-06, 30-08 or 264 casings. These were about three inches high with a rim around the base and a narrow neck. That meant they would easily stand on the linoleum floor in the living room. Dave and I would each take twenty-five shells to be our soldiers. We would bring out the wooden leaves for the kitchen table and set up the game. The leaves would be placed in a "V" shape at opposite ends of the living room. We could place the shells any way we wanted in the small part of the "V". With our jar of marbles, we would take turns rolling the marbles to knock down the other person's soldiers. The winner was the one who knocked all of the soldiers down first. It was a game I never tired of playing.

We played a card game called Touring. I know we wore out the cards way before we tired of the game. It was a game where you would draw a card and then throw one away. The cards had things on them like "25 miles" or "repair" or "gasoline" or "delay". The goal was to be the first to go a certain number of miles. I felt this game was a lot more fun and certainly more boyish than Old Maid.

When cousins came over we would play outside in the dark. We had a high pole by the old granary with a yard light on it. That gave us enough light to see but kept enough darkness so we were still able to hide. We would play "Anti-I-Over". In that game we had teams on each side of a building. The team on one side had to throw the ball over the building for the other side to catch it. The team that caught the ball would then run around the building and try to hit someone on the other team with the ball. If you hit someone, that person was out of the game. The team that lost all their players lost the game.

Anti-I-Over was fun but the most fun was Kick-the-Can. One person was "it". A can was placed in the middle of the yard. It would be a can about the size that government commodities came in. Those cans would be out of the house as soon as possible because Mom disliked them so much. The person who was "it" would then stand in the middle of the yard and count to 50. Everyone would hide and the game was on. The person who was "it" had to find people who were hiding and then run to the can and say their name. If they were successful the person who had been found had to go to jail. Sometimes the person who was found could get to the can first and kick it, then everyone in jail would be free. The game went on until everyone was in jail. Somebody then had to volunteer to be "it" and the game started all over again. I really liked this game because I thought I could hide well and run fast! The best place to hide was behind the old granary. There were so many cracks and holes in the siding you could position yourself on the dark side of it but find places where you could see through the building.

Dave and I would play cops and robbers often. We would use the old drill press, vice and anvil to make wooden guns. Then we would ride around the yard on make believe horses and shoot'm up! The hiding places for the bad guys could be the chicken house, the steel bins, the corn crib, the barn, the truck box or the trees to the east or the north. Sometimes those bad guys were really difficult to find but in the end we would prevail and capture them all. Those old guns would sure be fun to have today but they went up in smoke as did the entire farm. Maybe there were none left when the fire occurred but I would bet money that on some tucked away shelf there were old wooden guns lying around.

The age-old game of Monopoly was a favorite game. There would be times when we would play all day and then leave the game intact to continue another time. I am not sure we knew the rules but there were "Lee" rules that were followed and it seemed to be fun no matter if you ended up with a lot of properties or none at all. If someone ran out of money they could borrow from the bank. If the bank was low on funds a sibling would offer a loan. Why not, everyone needed to stay in the game if we were to have fun! I found out from Dad, as I got older, that in real life it was not such a good idea to borrow from the bank. Perhaps the lessons in Monopoly were not so good.

Dave, Ricky and I would play ball down by the corn crib. On the southeast corner of the farm yard there was a large grassy area that was never used. We would make a ball field of it and have the hitter stand against the corn crib so that we would not have to chase the ball. We could not use a real baseball because breaking the boards in the corn crib was not a good idea. We had a ball the same size as a baseball but it was rubbery rather than solid. One person would pitch, one would hit and one would field. Because there was only one fielder you had to hit the ball to the left of second base or be out. If we had time to play, we had to get on our bikes and ride the half mile to Ricky's. There were no phones or e-mail to make plans in the fifties! If Ricky was free he would bike back with us. Sometimes Ricky's mother, Eleanor, would have treats for us.

In the winter we would often put the two extra leaves in the kitchen table and play table tennis or as we would say ping-pong! It was challenging because the kitchen table was oval, with the leaves in it, so there were no corners to hit when we played. We always had to limit our playing to a time when Mom did not need the kitchen. With only a kitchen and a small living room, downstairs space was at a premium.

Another winter activity was hockey. We would trudge the half mile to the lake. With shovels in hand and skates around our necks we would find a place that was kind of smooth for an ice rink. Then with the snow shoveled to the sides we would sit on the ice, take our boots off and put on our skates. Our boots then became goals. Dave came up with the idea to make a hockey puck. He carefully cut round pieces of rubber out of an old inner tube. Then he glued them together and we had ourselves a great hockey puck. The downer was we did not think about the glue we used so about 30 minutes into our first hockey game the puck started to lose layers of rubber as the glue let loose in the below zero temperatures! No problem, we had brought our rubber ball, stashed in a pocket, for emergencies, so with a new puck that rolled faster we continued to play. The game would be over when our fingers or toes started to tell us the North Dakota temperatures were below zero.

We would play march around the house too. Mom loved to play the piano and we would beg her to play a particular song so we could march around the kitchen table, into the living room in a figure eight and back into the kitchen. The higher we could lift our legs, the more fun we had. Adding to the fun, we would sing at the top of our lungs to the beat of the march. I really should have thanked Mom for those marching skills as I used them in the high school marching band.

When I think of the games we played in my youth, it is amusing to reflect on the imaginations we had. There were no batteries needed, no electricity needed and not much money invested. It was just young bodies using their minds and physical abilities to have great fun. Sometimes as I sit with my French press coffee and gaze at the sunset or the sunrise I ask myself if maybe there is a lesson to be taken from the past.

Chapter Three

FREEZE OUT

North Dakota winters were cold when I was growing up. I think they still are cold but in the 50s, they were cold outside and cold inside too.

In the early 50s we had two ways to heat our house. In the kitchen we had the huge old cast iron cook stove and in the living room we had a kerosene burning stove. In the cook stove we burned corncobs, wood and coal in the reservoir and that created warmth for the kitchen, the downstairs bedroom and living room. The only problem was you had to feed the reservoir often. That meant a short time after you went to bed the heat stopped. In the living room kerosene stove we controlled the heat up or down with a knob on the right side. It sat on a metal tray which was a bit larger than the bottom of the stove. I think that metal tray was for any spillage of kerosene that may happen when the tank was being filled. There were several years when we needed to carry kerosene into the house, walk through the kitchen and then into the living room. We did that daily because during the coldest days it would burn at least five gallons. Later, maybe when I was nine or so, Dad splurged and put a fifty-five gallon barrel outside of the house on the north side. He then ran a line into the stove. That meant we could go for several days without carrying kerosene but it seemed like it was easier to just do it daily rather than carry several cans of kerosene at one time. I think the biggest advantage of having the barrel outside was we did not have to carry the fuel through the house and then pour it into the stove. If there was any chance of spillage the kerosene odor would permeate the entire house. Dad put the barrel outside so that would not happen.

The kerosene was kept in the old granary. Art, the fuel guy, would come and unload several barrels of kerosene and put them into the granary. I do not remember how he got them into the building but I am guessing he could back the truck up to the door and roll them out. We had a pump with a long pipe on the end. It was kind of like the pumps you see on a keg of beer but this was not pressurized so once the pump was in the barrel you had to screw it onto the top and then a small handle could be pumped up and down until the five gallon can was full. It was not important that the kerosene be kept in a dry place so most of the time the barrels sat in the front of the granary where snow could drift in but it was easy to get to. I remember trying to use the same gloves all the time because they would smell from handling the kerosene. I would leave them on the barrel in the granary.

I remember where Mom and Dad would sit in the winter time. Dad had a chair near the piano which was near the stove. It seemed as if every evening he would sit in the same chair rocking back and forth. He would read about loading shells, hunting or about photography. I really don't know anyone who was more "self-taught" than Dad. I am guessing he finished eighth grade about 1925 and but did not attend high school. He did go to an auto repair school in Aberdeen SD for two winters when he was in his early twenties. Mom would sit on the couch, on the north side of the living room, which was near the mounted deer head on the wall. Not that the deer head kept her warm, that is just where she sat while she knit or did some handiwork.

Actually the freeze out took place in the house, in my bedroom. My first memories of the upstairs bedrooms are when the boys' room was on the east and the girls' room was on the west. However, at some point, maybe about the time Dave started working away in the summers, we switched rooms and then the boys' room was on the west side of the house and the girls' room was on the east side. That meant it was not as easy for me to shoot blackbirds out of the window, but that was OK. I am not sure why we exchanged rooms. Maybe it was to be good to sister Helen. The east bedroom actually had been finished to some degree with dry wall. My room, the west room, was unfinished. It was unfinished in every way you could think.

As you walked past the curtain that hid the five gallon pail toilet and into my bedroom there was a wall on the right for about five feet. On the left was an open space that led to the attic. The attic was a small space the length of the house from east to west. At the highest place in the attic, when you first crawled in, it may have been four feet high. It angled back about six feet to nothing as the roof sloped down the south side of the house. There were no valuable items in the attic.

Dad kept his hunting and camera magazines there amid boxes and boxes of nothing.

As you walked past the attic opening there was a long rod suspended from the rafters and that extended to the window. That was where my clothes hung. A large closet, as the rod was maybe ten feet long, but not too fancy!! On the north side of the room was my bed. It was an old iron bed with a spring that was old and a mattress that was perhaps older. By the bed was a table that had my clock radio on with the cord extending around and under the bed to an outlet. The walls of the room were simply the wall studs of the second floor. There was no dry wall or anything that would make for a comfortable room. When you looked up towards the ceiling you saw the roof trusses and all the boards where the shingles were attached. The shingle nails sticking through the boards looked like it could be some kind of torture board! To this day I often wonder how the house was kept dry. I do not remember Dad ever working on the roof. I actually have dreams from time to time where I am working on a leaky roof of a house. There was no heat upstairs and I don't think there were storm windows either but I may be wrong about that. It would have been so easy for Dad to cut a hole in the floor of the girls' room and boys' room and that would have let enough warmth up to make it kind of nice but maybe he thought that would use too much kerosene. Whatever his reasoning was he never shared it but you can bet he didn't sleep there either. I would keep warm by not moving and staying under several quilts. Later in high school Mom bought me an electric blanket and I would set records when I ran upstairs, undressed and scurried under the quilts. It was extra nice when Mom would go upstairs and turn it on before I came home from a late basketball game. In the dead of winter my radio clock would not work because it was so cold. Sometimes I would lie in bed on a Saturday morning and try to count the frost covered nails on a particular board! There were two windows on the west, one small one and one large one. They would frost over so you could not see out. When you put your hand on the walls, these were actually the boards that the siding was attached to; you could feel the cold as if you were outside.

I am sure there were times the barn, with the cattle, cats and dog in it, was warmer than my bedroom but then I admit I never considered sleeping in the barn. I have not thought much about our winter activities but maybe one of the reasons I loved to go outside sledding or just romping in the snow is there may not have been much difference in the temperature outside and the temperature in my bedroom.

Chapter Four

DECISIONS

Every person can remember decisions in life that make a big difference. Sometimes a decision can be life changing. Many times in my youth and in my adult life there have been decisions that impact the present and then there are decisions that impact the future. Regardless whether they are big or small, there are always decisions that linger in the mind and tell you some secrets of your inner most being!

Mom and Dad were off to take pictures some place so that left Dave and me home on this Farmers Union night. That was unthinkable. Mom and Dad always went to Farmers Union meetings. They were held monthly at Wood Lake School and they seemed so important to me. Well there never was any old or new business to speak of but there was always a program and goodies afterwards. For the program Helen may sing, Mom and Dad may sing, Olaf may play the violin and always Rollof would raise his hand and request to sing "Sing Your Way Home" first. That was kind of a ritual and when he did that everyone would laugh and then Mom would bang out the tune for everyone to sing. In midsummer there usually was time for the boys and the dads to play a ball game. For me, the ball game was almost better than the goodies. The only reason the goodies trumped the ball game was because Mom would always allow me to dip several sugar lumps in her coffee and suck on them—so delicious. Regardless, Dave and I were home alone one warm summer night with the instructions to walk to the Farmers Union meeting. After all the school was only a mile and a half from our farm. As we headed out we thought it was kind of late and why not just jump in the big red truck and drive? So off we go in 'Big Red", only a mile and a half to Wood Lake School and it was a fun ride. Bad decision, as Dad had failed to tell why we should walk. He had begun to winterize things on the farm and had already drained the water out of the radiator of the truck. In the days following our joy ride, Dad took the engine apart and overhauled it. We did not get scolded for our misbehavior.

When I was in early grade school, I would often drive the Ford tractor because it was small and easy to handle. All I had to do when I shifted gears was push down with my left foot, shift and let the pedal up. I could not drive the International M because to shift that you had to push ahead with your left foot and it was hard. Dave or Dad would always do the work when the M was needed. I was shocked one day when for some reason Dave could not work in the field so Dad told me to go down south, we farmed eighty acres of Uncle Jim's land there, and disc the thirty acres that we were summer fallowing that year. The fields down south were divided into two thirty acres plots and a twenty acre hay field. The hay land was native prairie that we hayed and the other two were into crops. Dad would rotate the plots so that every other year a plot was not planted and we kept it black all summer. That gave the land a rest and I think it was a great way to farm. We would plow the field in the fall and then the next summer we would disc several times so that the weeds would not start. On this day the weeds needed to be killed and Dad sent me down to work. He showed me how I needed to pull a rope and back up to engage the disc and then pull the rope and drive forward to disengage it. Off I went to do my work. Dad told me that I should finish before sundown so when I finished I should leave the disc there and drive the tractor home. I was proud but apprehensive as I had not driven the M very much. I knew I could do it. I arrived at the field, engaged the disc and made half a round. At that point I had to make a decision. Could I turn with the disc engaged or did I need to disengage it at each turn? I tried to turn with it engaged and it made this farrow in a circle and I thought that could not be good so I disengaged it and made the next half trip. As the sun began to set I was maybe two thirds finished and I could not figure out why Dad said I should be done, but what could I do. Our family rule, and for sure I would never break the rules, was when the sun sets you are done working. Dad could not figure out why I did not finish the field until I told him that I did a really good job because I did not make those ugly farrows of dirt on the turns! I found out that I had made a bad decision, the disc was supposed to stay engaged all the time. I never did understand why Dad did not tell me that prior to my field work.

Haying was always a fun time for me. Before I was old enough to be in the stack I had the great job of driving the Ford tractor all over the field and gathering up the loose hay that the stacker would miss. We pulled the rake behind the Ford. The rake was a horse rake that Dad had modified. It had a step that you would push down and the rake would dump. We fixed up a rope from the step to the tractor. I would drive all over the field and when the rake was full of hay I would drive over a bunch of hay and trip the rake. I could do this all day long and it was a fun time but I had to add something. For some reason I loved to start the Ford. It had a key and all you had to do is turn the key to on and press a button. I figured out a way that I could start the tractor often. Every time I would see a field mouse I would stop the tractor, turn it off and try to catch the mouse. Then I would need to start it again and off I would go. One time for some reason the tractor would not start and Dad was not a happy camper! He asked me why I shut it off so honest me, I told him. I found out that I had made a bad decision.

One of the hardest decisions I had to make occurred about when I was about ten. We had church and Sunday school every other week because the pastor had three churches. He would preach in town every Sunday and would alternate his two rural parishes. Mom was my Sunday school teacher and she did a great job. Chuckie and I seemed to be the smartest ones in the class although Gay and the Tosse girl were okay too! I was proud of never missing Sunday school for any reason. I had perfect attendance for two years plus and I had no intention of missing anytime soon. Dad had taken Ronald to Missouri for surgery. Ronald would be in the hospital for several days so Dad came home and would return to get him in a few days. He came over to me Friday when I was putting gas in the Ford after dinner and said he was leaving the next day to get Ronald. He asked me if I would like to go with him. Well, that was an opportunity that I could not pass up except when I asked him when we would be home he said Sunday night. My face almost fell to the ground. That meant missing Sunday school for the first time in more than two years. How could I give up my plan of having perfect attendance for the third straight year? I think Mom gave us little pins for perfect attendance and I wanted that pin. I also wanted to hear the lesson, see Chucky and be part of the rivalry between the boys and girls to see who could answer the most questions. I went into the house and talked to Mom. She assured me that she did not want me to miss class either but I would have a lot of fun going to get Ronald. It took me a long time before I decided that perfect attendance was really not so important and going with Dad to Missouri was a really big deal. Getting Ronald would be the thing to do, so off we went to Missouri Saturday morning and I had a great time. That was a good decision.

Today many of those decisions seem trivial and unimportant now but growing up they were off the charts in importance. I think the way I went about making decisions carried over into adult life and has allowed me to make good decisions most of the time. Today I am glad that Sunday school was that important to me, even if all my reasons were not totally pure!

Chapter Five

THE FALL BURN: EXCITING! FUN! DANGEROUS!

I had mixed feelings when I was growing up on the farm. I loved the Ford tractor and all that I could do with it. I enjoyed the lake and the time we spent swimming, fishing and water skiing. Most of the animals were my pets. We had names for all the milk cows. One of my favorites was Lumpy. She had some kind of lump on the side of her face so we were really creative in names! I remember playing and working in the wide open spaces and it just seemed like I could run forever, dream of things that "could be" and just be who I wanted to be.

On the other hand I must have said a million times, "I will never be a farmer". I think that was because all of our machinery was old and run down, I would say everything would have qualified for antique status. It seemed that Dad had stood still in time as all the other farmers advanced in what they had and how they did things. I had no concept of the money part and I remember hating harvest because the oats and barley were so itchy I almost went crazy. There were times that a person had to be on the combine or truck and the grain chaff with all the thistle flowers would engulf you as it were a dust storm. I hated that part yet of course that was the main source of income for our family. How could one hate the part that supported us all year?

I guess you could excuse a boy who was into play and not work and was living out his youth years before adulthood came along. I would make the calves pets and then they would grow up and we would sell them. So I disliked the things that were our source of income yet I was always aware that we had little or no money. In high school I didn't even dare shut the car off on some lonely road when I had a date! If I did I would be afraid the car battery would give out and it would not start. Well I actually had good reason for that fear but I will not go into that. Most of my clothes were hand me downs and I had to try hard to look like others. Actually Dave and I tried really hard. There was a time when the "in" thing was to have a crew cut and have the hair stand straight up. Somehow we were able to get Dad to buy us some Butch Wax, a concoction that made your hair stiff. We would then wear nylon stockings on our heads at night to make our hair stand up. That did the trick; the hair would be trained to stand up. In hind sight, it was a goofy thing to do but we did what we thought would make us like others!

In grade school and in high school I remember getting on the bus to go home and thinking how fun it would be to live in town. I knew the boys in town would be playing ball after school and I would be home maybe working in the field or milking cows. Most of the time in high school I had football or basketball practice but in the spring I would ride the bus home right after school. I would see the guys and gals walking towards downtown and I wondered what they did as I rode the bus for the next hour. I had many mixed feelings about my life but there were also many good things too.

Of all the good things on the farm, one of the best was the fall burn. We would burn the ditches along the half mile road that led to our farm and we would also burn most of the sloughs on our farmland to the west and to the east. Dad had a great way to light the fires. He made a long pipe with a bend on the end. He would stuff material into the bent end. The material would be a rag from an old shirt or pants. Then he would fill the copper pipe with kerosene, letting the kerosene soak into the rag which plugged the end of the pipe. We could then light the rag with a long farmers match and simply walk along the ditch. As we walked along the ditch or around the slough, little flames would drop out of the pipe and start the burn. When we had walked the half mile down to the main road the entire ditch was burning. It was a fun thing to do but of course Dad always emphasized that it had to be the right kind of weather and if there was any wind, it had to be from the right direction. As we walked south to the main road our pasture was on the west and for sure we did not want to burn that.

When the ditches were burned we would usually burn some of the larger sloughs on our land. That was the most fun. They usually were full of tall weeds and dried up grass. That meant the fire was bigger, the smoke was thicker and the smell was better! For some reason I loved the smell of burning dry grass and those tall weeds. It was extra special fun when the slough had these tall hollow reeds. I could then rescue some of them and light the end. For a time I could pretend that I was an adult with this fat cigar in my mouth. That made me feel so big but of course I would not let much of the smoke get into my mouth.

Dave and I almost had two disasters with fire. On our land to the west, we were plowing shortly after we had finished combining the rye. There was too much straw so we decided to burn the stubble so the plows would not always plug up. It got away from us and the fire headed towards the combine that was still parked in the field. It was touch and go with a lot of sweat but we were able to extinguish it before the combine was harmed. The other time it was more dangerous as we were plowing the rye field east of our farm. Again, there was so much straw that our plows were plugging up and making it impossible to get any work done. Time for another burn but this time there could have been even more severe consequences. As the burn began, it became clear that we had no idea that when straw burns it makes a bigger and bigger fire. That in turn creates its own wind and the fire can get out of hand quickly. The fire jumped our dirt line and headed straight north toward neighbor Bert's wheat field. Bert was usually a bit late with his farm work so the field was not cut and it looked to be a bumper crop! Again, we sweat, prayed, yelled and worked perhaps harder than ever and were just able to stop it short of the dry creek bed. If we had not been able to stop it, I don't want to know what might have happened except to say we may still be paying for it!

The fall burn; it was a time on the farm that was magical in many senses. The fascination of fire, the smell of the smoke, the adventure of hollow reeds used as cigars, all melded into an adventure that somehow made our antiquated farm life livable.

*Our house after I left home. Our wind charger had
been replaced by a TV antenna in 1962*

Chapter Six

FAMILY FINANCES

Our main money crop was wheat and this looked to be a bumper year. The golden ripples of wheat had been cut into windrows. It would be just one more day of drying before the combine would swallow them up and separate the wheat from the chaff. Then the golden kernels would be trucked home to be sold at a later date. It appeared that we would have a good winter.

Mom and Dad were thrilled. Money was always high in demand and short in supply. However, this year hopefully the tables would be turned. The price of wheat had recently gone up to $2.10 a bushel. Dad figured that a conservative estimate would be thirty bushels per acre. That meant an acre would bring in at least $63 and for the thirty acre field the income would probably exceed two thousand dollars. A new car could be had for less than that. Dad and Mom were not going to buy a new car but there were many needs and maybe, just maybe, this was the year they could purchase some things they needed.

It was Thursday and Dad felt we could finish harvesting the field by late afternoon on Saturday. The middle steel bin, the largest bin we had, was clean and the elevator was up, ready to transport wheat into its gut. Dad walked out of the yard, beyond the house, and into the field. He took a couple heads of wheat, shelled them into his hand and examined them. Then he bit into one and tasted it. Tomorrow we can harvest he said as we walked back to the house. There was an air of anticipation and excitement surrounding the entire farm.

By noon the combine had been readied, the truck was set to rumble and everything was in place. Mom came out of the house as Dad and I were changing the screen in the back of the combine. We needed different screens for different crops and a few days earlier we had harvested barley. A wheat screen had to be put in place. Mom said she had the radio on and a possible storm was coming in late afternoon. After fastening the last screw on the screen, Dad stood up and walked west beyond the barn. There, on the horizon, the sun had disappeared and black clouds approached.

No doubt, we were going to get rain but the eminent storm hinted there may be more than rain. The neat windrows of wheat could endure rain. The rain would reduce the quality some but it still would be an excellent crop. However, if those dark clouds harbored hail it could be disaster. As the wind became stronger and daylight disappeared, concern turned to apprehension. Then it hit. The force of the wind, the rain and the hail threatened to damage the buildings and perhaps even break the windows. Dad became silent and Mom quietly shed tears as the storm raged on for a time. Then, almost as if someone reached down and lifted a veil the rain stopped, the hail ceased, the air became calm and the sun peaked through the clouds.

There on our front lawn glistened a layer of hail stones, some larger than golf balls. I knew from watching Mom and Dad that it was not good but yet as a kid I delighted in those shiny stones everywhere. In a voice that was almost a whisper, Dad said he would walk out to the wheat field. Mom followed but several steps behind. Mom and Dad knew what they would find. There, row after row after row curving around the field were wide bands of shelled wheat lying on the rain soaked earth. It was almost as if someone had taken dollar bills, shred them into tiny bits, and neatly placed them in rows going round and round the thirty acre field. There was nothing to recover. There were our new shoes, our school supplies, winter coats, Christmas presents and more lying in rows, nothing would be salvaged.

I remember the figure of seven hundred dollars. That was what Mom and Dad had to spend in the next twelve months. That had to pay for everything. There was gas, there was spring seed, school supplies for four kids, food to put on the table and countless other needs. If imagination and thriftiness was ever in order, it was needed for us in the coming year.

Mom was in charge of food and she did a masterful job. Perhaps this was the time I remember having to eat boiled wheat berries for breakfast. I hated them but maybe they made me strong! There would be deer meat in the fall. At that time perhaps could Dad could shoot two deer, Ronald one and they even purchased a tag for Janet. Beef would be sold, not butchered. We qualified for free hot lunch at school which made Mom ashamed. I never did ask Dad how he managed to work the fields the next spring or put the crop in but my guess is he worked on borrowed money from the bank. I know one day several years later he asked me if I wanted to go to Lidgerwood as he was going to pay off a car loan of five hundred dollars. He said that loan had been on the books for many years. I am sure this was one of those years that the boxes of clothes from California came in handy.

We received government commodities which Mom hated. I remember she was ashamed to get them and would make sure they were stored out of sight. They consisted of flour, powdered milk, cheese, and other items. The cream that I put on bread, mush or pancakes was not eaten much but rather was sold in Cayuga to Bennie Flash. Mr. Flash would buy eggs and cream from us. The government cheese and powdered milk made canned suckers and boiled wheat berries almost good. I am not sure the government commodities were so bad but knowing how Mom was so ashamed of them probably influenced my taste.

Many years later, in the nineties, Dad had an auction sale in Veblen. He still owned 80 acres of land where the farm had been but he had his house in town and its contents auctioned off. The check he received for everything, house and belongings, was under $10,000.

Chapter Seven

HIGH SCHOOL DAYS

In grade school I was kind of a big fish in a tiny bowl. I could hit the ball farther than anyone else, I read more books than anyone else and good grades came easily for me but in the fall of 1961 I was in for a new experience.

When I started fourth grade I left Wood Lake School, which was a mile and a half from our farm. I got on the bus to start school in Cayuga where there were twenty-four students in my classroom. It is a bit of a stretch to say twenty-four students because some of the kids in my classroom were in school and participated in things but they really could not be classified as students. Maybe they were more like unwilling hostages forced to attend school during the day. Anyway, it was a huge shock for me. My one room, eight grades, twelve student environment became a multiple room place with about one hundred twenty-five students with a hot lunch program and bathrooms with flush toilets! If you included kindergarten, there were thirteen grades, which are more grades than students in Wood Lake the previous year. When I entered seventh grade the high school students began the trek to Forman, to attend Sargent Central High School. That meant I moved up to the top floor and became one of the "top dogs". I was tall for my age and I found athletics an easy endeavor so there I was, kind of king of the hill and loving every minute of it.

During the summer of nineteen sixty-one I thought a lot about high school. My brother Ronald and my sister Janet had gone to Lidgerwood High School in the early fifties. They had gone to college and Ronald graduated with his four year degree and Janet with her two year degree. Ronald was teaching and Janet was married and her husband John was teaching. Sister Joan had graduated a year ago and was working in Fargo while Dave would be a senior in high school in the fall. Only sister Helen was still in grade school. I felt that I was going into the big time and I was somewhat afraid.

Even though good grades had come rather easily for me in grade school I really was not that interested in studying. I was more interested in playing some kind of ball, any kind of ball. I had played basketball for two years in grade school and actually had done quite well after I learned that you couldn't stand in the lane all the time, you couldn't take a step without dribbling the ball and once you came over the half line with the ball you couldn't go back again! I could shoot the ball pretty well as I practiced that often at home in the hay barn or outside by the light pole. Dribbling, well that was kind of a challenge. I do not know how I found out but sometime during the summer I learned that football started a week before school. I suspect Mr. Hanson, the football coach from Sargent Central, contacted Mr. Murray. He coached Little League baseball and basketball in Cayuga. Mr. Hanson probably asked if there would be any ninth grade boys coming in who may be football players. In early August I received a letter that football practice started a week before school. I suspect Dad knew that too but he did not say anything to me or encourage me in any way. The Monday before school started came and went as I sat on the farm thinking I wanted to play football. I had never played football but I really wanted to try out for the team. Tuesday came and it was the same, my thoughts were about football but I dared not ask Dad. Finally, Tuesday night I gathered up the courage to approach Dad as he sat in his rocking chair reading a hunting magazine. I asked, "Can I go out for the football team this fall?" Without looking up he said, "I suppose" and then he went on reading his magazine. I then had to ask another question as I knew practice had already started. "Can I start practice this week?" I asked. That got his attention and after a brief pause he said he would take me to Forman the next day.

I had no idea what I should bring or what I should wear but I jumped in the car with Dad Wednesday morning feeling excited, nervous and apprehensive. When we arrived in Forman I saw there were several guys out on the field with an older man, who I thought must be the coach. I was so glad when Dad offered to walk with me out onto the field towards the coach. Dad told him I was interested in trying out for the football team. The coach's eyes lit up as he eyed this 5 foot, 11 inch freshman farm boy who looked every bit the raw football size player high school teams cherish. Here was this freshman who was as big as most guys out on the field and Mr. Hanson was delighted to walk me to the locker room for equipment. Mr. Hanson led us into the school locker which smelled like it needed some fresh air and said I would have to buy some football shoes but I did not need them for today. He said most of the equipment had been handed out but he did scrounge around enough to find a practice jersey, some pants that were a bit too small, knee pads, thigh pads, shoulder pads and whatever else was needed. I did not even know where to put all the pads. Dad left me standing there with the word he would be outside when practice was finished. I am glad I do not know what I looked like that day. It seemed like everyone was having a good time but for me there was this knot in my stomach. I finally came across Larry, my best friend in grade school, and then things seemed a bit better.

Football became my favorite high school sport. I quickly learned that even though I could not run faster than most I could hit harder than most and could read things in front of me very well. I started on the football team for three years and served as captain in my senior year. At the end of my senior year the assistant coach came to me and said he had talked to his college coach in Jamestown ND who was interested in me playing college football the next fall. At that time I was not interested in a teacher's college so I said I was not interested. So what did I do in the future years, I became a teacher!

I also enjoyed basketball. As a freshman I started on the freshman team which went undefeated and also on the "B" team. A friend, John, and I even got to suit up for two varsity games which was unheard of for freshman. I think I got in for thirty seconds or so and I was thrilled. For the next three years I played varsity basketball and started as a senior while my friend John and I served as co-captains. The highlight of basketball was going to the state tournament as a junior.

I played the game I loved the most, baseball, when I was a freshman but our school dropped the sport the next fall so I then participated in track. Track was not very much fun for me as Dad wanted me to come home after school in the spring to work in the fields. That meant I had to practice by myself during study hall. I would go to the track meets and actually did very well with the javelin and discus throw but not being able to be with the "guys" at practice took much of the fun out of it.

During high school I earned eleven letters in four sports. It was sports that I lived for during those four years. I did not have more ability or skills than my teammates but there was always something in me that enabled me to be successful on the court or on the field. It may have been the hours of playing ball against the south barn wall or the hours of shooting the tiny rubber ball in the hay barn. I think more than anything, athletic ability was a family trait. Dad boxed and played baseball, Ronald was good at sports and Dave was a natural. The one thing I remember being good at was having a court sense or field sense that often gave me an advantage over my opponent.

Aside from sports there was one situation when I was a freshman that changed my entire high school days and carried into adulthood. Mr. Hanson, the football coach, also taught shop. Back in the sixties shop meant woodworking. All of the boys took shop and all the girls took cooking and sewing! Boys did not take cooking and girls did not take shop!! I did not like shop and I suspect it was because I did not have money to buy wood to make anything. Mr. Hanson saw that and asked a friend, John and me if we would like to make some picnic tables for some of the teachers. Not only would the teachers buy the wood but they would pay us for building them! I know that tiny little insight, by Mr. Hanson, not only ignited an interest in woodworking that stayed with me all my life but it also gave me a little money plus we got an "A" in the class. I sometimes think about what my life would have been like if my dad would have exercised insights like that!

High school days also brought about some changes on the home front. During my sophomore year, my brother Ronald came to visit with a big box on the front seat of his car. It was a television, something I had wanted for a long time. Now I could watch the Saturday afternoon baseball game of the week with Dizzy Dean. With our hastily erected antenna, the snowy picture became kind of okay. Mom and Dad fell in love with Mr. North Dakota, Lawrence Welk, as he featured the Lennon Sisters and Larry Hooper!

We got new band uniforms for our big
trip to Indianapolis for the 500 race

There were many other experiences in high school that were fun. Our band trips to places like Canada, the Indianapolis 500 race and so many homecoming parades were always fun. Our elementary school did not have music so when I arrived in high school, band was a new experience. I started out playing the baritone but changed to the sousaphone, we called it a tuba, in my sophomore year. I never became very accomplished but it was a fun activity. One of my excuses for not playing very well was bringing a sousaphone home to practice seemed like too much work The chorus concerts and Christmas events, the proms and actually many of the long, long bus rides all made high school a wonderful time in my life. I am forever thankful for the blessings that God gave me, so that this country boy with hand-me-down clothes and little money could have such a great experience in high school.

Chapter Eight

ICONS OF THE FARM

Nobody in the country had a wind charger on top of their house with us being the exception. You could identify our farm for miles away by that wind charger that went around and around when the North Dakota winds blew, which was most of the time. There were four iron legs attached to the roof of our house, two on the south slope and two on the north slope. The blades were on some kind of device that allowed it to rotate with the wind. That old antiquated charger provided electricity for a radio and one working lightbulb in the living room. As the evening worn on and the batteries' charge waned, the radio sound would become muffled before it went off. The lightbulb would dim, dim some more, and then darkness meant bedtime!

After the storm, when we finally dared venture out of the school, we looked west across Uncle Obert's field and knew our farm was not the same; no wind charger appeared above the tree line. We raced home to find a twisted mess of metal that looked like it could be transformed into art but could not give of itself any longer. Perhaps it knew that "electricity" had invaded the Lee Farm and it was no longer needed!

Maybe the best icon of the farm was "Big Red", our beloved truck. It was a 1935 version with a flathead 8 engine which growled when you drove! The unique thing about it was it had a hoist on it. We could back up to the auger, start to unload grain and as the box began to empty we would hoist up the front of the grain box so we had to shovel very little. I think the hoist was a modern item but the truck—not so modern. The hoist was one item that we had and most farmers did not. I never did figure out why or how that happened. Even though it was old we used it all the time. I think I could almost write a book about "Big Red". Dave and I had great conversations while sitting in the truck out in the harvest field. We loved to race across the field, pick choke cherries and then race back and have a choke cherry seed spitting contest as we sat in the truck. The front windshield cranked out, almost like an exotic sports car. One time Dave and I took it to Uncle Halvor's and on the way we met another truck. Dave moved over as far as he could but the other truck just kind of came down the middle of the road. The corner of our box nicked the corner of theirs and scared us half to death. Either the other guy could not see, his truck was too large or the road was too narrow. I will always remember "Big Red" but really for a farm truck it was quite small.

Jayhawk, the name, was stamped on the front iron of the hay stacker. It was one of a kind. The stacker attached to the narrow front end of the M tractor. There was a cast iron hub, about the size of a ten inch dinner plate, which fit over a heavy ball attached to the front end of the tractor. From the end that fastened to the tractor, two angle irons went up and came down in the form of triangles. At about fifteen feet or so they met two more angle irons coming from the front. On the front end was a huge bucket that had long wooden teeth. There was a long iron pull rod from the bucket to where Dad sat on the tractor. When he had the bucket full of hay, he would drive towards the stack and pull on the long rod. The bucket would rise in the air until he released the handle of the rod. Then he would push the rod and the bucket would dump the hay. Dad would then back up and as the bucket touched the ground it would fall back into place and lock. Our stacks were bigger and higher than any in the country and I would say the people forming the stacks did a perfect job!

The Ford tractor was a big little tractor. It was metal gray with red trim and it was the easiest thing on the farm to drive. I know everyone was driving it when we were six or so. All you had to do was push down on the clutch and shift gears. We had several pieces of equipment that attached to the draw bar like the plow, the bucket, the disc and the mower. We used the Ford to plow, to pull the drag, to windrow the crops, to pull the rock wagon and the hay rack. At least once it was even used to transport Ronald to Geneseo in the winter when the roads were impassable and he needed to catch a ride to high school in Lidgerwood. Nobody near our farm had a Ford tractor. They all had John Deere, Case, Minneapolis Moline, Oliver, Allis Chalmers or Massey Fergusons. Nobody had a 1947 Ford 8N like ours!

Maybe more than any other thing on the farm, the creek provided entertainment all year long. I am not sure a creek qualifies as an icon but I can't really leave it out. It came onto our farm on the south end of our land. It entered under the bridge and meandered through the pasture and exited northeast of our house by another bridge. It gave us hours of playing in the water, walking through the tall grass looking for pheasants, the challenge of finding a way across when it was high, fishing by the rock dam below the three holer, sailing wooden boats in the current and countless hours of just walking along it looking for things in the water. I would say more than anything else, the creek identified our farm. No place else could you find a snake rock or tiny little creatures in the mud or fish caught in the rocks. In the spring, for a short time, it would be a raging river but by mid-summer it would be this gentle, winding tiny creek with water holes and mud holes everywhere.

Perhaps one of my favorite icons, a great one for sure, would be the gas pump. It stood like a beacon as people turned into our driveway and drove up to the house. The gas pump was where we parked the tractors at noon, where Dad parked the combine to oil the chains and grease the pulleys and where, in high school we would back up to put in gas before we left on a date. With its ten gallon glass bulb on top of its red base, which was a cast iron tapered cylinder, it identified this farm as the place where six kids grew up, only to spread their wings and fly far away. It was a sad day for Dad when a cousin came to visit and backed into the gas pump. Did he scold her? No, but he was upset for a long time.

I will always wonder if any of us kids would have returned to the farm if Dad had been a real farmer instead of a hunter and a photographer who happened to live on a farm. I will never know and perhaps it is not very important because the icons of the farm will live on forever and the "what if" things seem unimportant now.

*Carmen, the
great fisherman*

Chapter Nine

FISHING

Here I am in my sixties and doing many things. I enjoy biking, walking, tennis, woodworking, photography and many other activities that keep me more than busy. However, one of my favorite pastimes growing up was fishing.

I think one of the main reasons we went fishing was to catch something to eat. That would have been Dad's objective but it certainly was not mine. The only fish we ever caught were perch, bullheads, crappies and northern pike. People loved bullheads, in fact small towns would have bullhead fries but we never ate them. I actually caught a bullhead from time to time but I would always throw it back. If you have never seen a bullhead just think of a "bull head" and you know what it looks like. No matter what the fish was, there were bones, bones and more bones. I did not even know there was such a thing as "fileting" a fish. Until I was an adult I thought the only thing anybody ever did was clean a fish, take the scales off and fry it. I assumed that any time you ate fish it was normal that you would pick out bones, put a bit in your mouth and then pick out more bones as you chewed and finally say a prayer before you swallowed, hoping that no bones would get stuck in your throat. I imagined that maybe parents served fish once a week to the kids so that they could get the kids to eat more slowly and maybe even persuade them to share what was going on in their lives during the meal! Today I really enjoy having fish for a meal but growing up it was something I dreaded. I still can feel and taste the fish as it slowly, so slowly, churned and tumbled and became mushy in my mouth before I dared to swallow.

So fishing, for me, was not about bringing food home but rather about going someplace with Dad, eating some food that we did not get very often and just being outside on the lake in a boat. We did not have a boat of our own but there were times when Dad would borrow Uncle Halvor's outboard motor and then he would rent a boat at the marina. That was the most fun.

There were four kinds of fishing that I remember. They were:

Get up early, before the sun came up, and go to Silver Lake or the west end of Lake Tewaukon to cast for northerns.

Dig worms or buy minnows and go to Lake Traverse in South Dakota to fish for crappies. When we did that, it was rent a boat or fish from shore. An added plum sometimes was when Dad would stop at the store and buy saltines and sardines. Yummy. We would also go to Lake Traverse in the winter and ice fish. It seemed like we always came home with a bucket full of crappies. Of course more fish meant more bones!

Another kind of fishing was when I would walk or ride the little bike the half mile to Lake Tewaukon and just fish for perch so I could put them in my corral and play with them. That of course is another story.

The last kind of fishing was later when I would sometimes go with Dad to the hills south of the farm. There were several lakes where we would fish for northerns. Of the many lakes in the hills, I remember Dad's favorites were Roy Lake, Clear Lake and Long Lake. There also was a buffet kind of restaurant at Roy Lake where Dad and Mom loved to take us when we visited them as adults. They thought the "all you could eat chicken" was the best ever!

When I think about fishing as a child it was not about the fish at all. Really what I yearned for was time to be with Dad. Mom and Dad certainly had different roles in my childhood. Mom was always there for me. She was the one who made the meals, she was the one who took care of the scrapes and bruises, and she was the encouraging one always. It was Mom who would ask if I wanted to go to town with Dad. It was Dad, if he did not want company, who would take me, crying, behind the house and with a sharp slap on the behind tell me to not cry about such things and to be a big boy. I wanted to spend time with Dad. Not only did I want to spend time with him but I wanted him to teach me, encourage me and make me feel useful when I was with him. That really did not happen very often. I would beg him to hit fly balls to me on Sunday afternoon. When he did give in I thought I was the luckiest boy in the world. Then if he would happen to mention a good catch or a nice throw I would almost bust the buttons on my shirt!

So fishing, well it was fun, but to stand by Dad as I cast the Dare Devil lure, or to share those saltines and sardines with him was great. To be able to show him I could bait the hook or get the fish off of the hook was important to me. One time we were having a picnic but I had brought my fishing pole along. As Mom and Dad were enjoying a bite to eat I was lazily casting my line off shore and dreaming about that big fish. All of a sudden I actually had this northern on my line. I reeled it in and marched up the steep incline with the fish as if I was the biggest, the best and most famous fisherman in the world. It was a day to remember.

As I write about my fishing days with Dad I suddenly have the urge to grab that rod and reel from the garage wall and head out to the Gulf. Maybe, just maybe, there is another memory to catch!

Chapter Ten

A MIRACLE

People have said many things about miracles. Some expect God to perform miracles all the time and when He doesn't they don't understand. Others really do not believe God works that way so when something really unusual happens they try to explain it in a human way. You hear that was luck or he was in the right place at the right time or the situation really wasn't what it was said to be.

However, the most important miracle for me actually happened when I was in elementary school and at the time I did not even realize it. It happened over a period of a couple of years. When I look back at it there simply is no explanation for what happened in my life except God in his love and wisdom and for unknown reasons, decided to heal me of stuttering.

I was painfully shy growing up. That probably contributed to my speech problem. I remember one day after I had finished fourth grade Dad asked if I would like to ride to town with him. I always jumped at the chance to be with Dad and I knew that going to town could possibly mean a candy bar or even a hamburger at Cecil's café in Cayuga. We arrived in Cayuga and parked across the street from Kiefer's hardware and implement store. I loved to go into the store and look at equipment and hardware items but Dad said I should stay in the car and of course I did. I was disappointed and angry. Why he wanted me to stay in the car was and still is a mystery but what Dad said, you did. As I sat there I started to play with my baseball cards. I seldom went any place without them. I pulled them out of my pocket and started to sort them by the player I liked the most to those who were less important to me. I was so engrossed with my cards that I did not see her right away. Walking towards me was Mrs. Wohler, one of the teachers from school. I knew she would see me and say "Hi". I was so afraid of talking to her that I quickly jumped over the seat and flattened myself on the back floor of the car until I was sure she was past. There was no reason to avoid her except I was almost afraid to talk to adults. I remember when we would go places; I always made sure I was close to Mom or Dad so that I would not have to talk to people myself.

I remember many details of my stuttering. I know adults who are stutterers and it is not an easy issue to deal with. There was no special education in those days so getting help from the school was a non-issue. When I look back, that may have been a huge blessing. My stuttering was at its worst when I was in the sixth grade. I would have sleepless nights if I knew I might be asked to stand in front of the class the next day. One day my teacher, Mrs. Fox, called on me to get up in front of the class and give an oral book report. I remember standing in front of everyone. My desk was in the middle of the second row from the windows. The teacher's desk was in front of the first two rows. I picked up my short report with a clammy hand and slowly walked to the front of the room. Even though I was only in the sixth grade I was physically mature for my age but at that moment I felt two feet tall. I know I was sweating, my throat was like chalk and I am sure my face was contorted a bit. I stood there, it seemed like an eternity and my mind went blank. My mind flashed back to the time when I stood in the Lidgerwood gym naked, waiting to weigh in for boxing lessons. I silently asked the Lord to deliver me from this situation! I stared at the paper, I stared at my classmates and opened my mouth but no words or sound came forth. After what seemed like an eternity, Mrs. Fox finally said I could sit down. With a red face, moist, clammy hands and perhaps dark stains under my arm pits, I slowly walked to my desk which seemed to be a mile away. I did hand in my written report and received credit for it but I do not remember if Mrs. Fox took points off for the lack of my oral report.

I think my size had something to do with me getting over my speech problem. It sounds a bit crazy but I believe it helped. I know that grade school kids can be mean with words and physical things but because I was big for my age and strong as well, I never was teased about my speech. One time, three boys roughed me up as I got on the bus after school but over the next few days everything was worked out so nobody ever attempted that again! Back in the 1950's arguments were often settled with a wrestling match at recess time and nobody wanted to wrestle me. There surely were many reasons for growing out of my stuttering but my size helped. I was never mean to others but I was firm in who I was and I believed I had the right to be treated fairly.

I believe the lack of school intervention, the patience of my parents and God's grace slowly over two years dissolved my speech problem into a non-issue. It sounds strange but the fact that the school had no assistance was really a big help. There was no attention brought to it and there was no separating me from the class to go and get special treatment. My parents knew nothing about solving a stuttering problem but they tried some things that may have helped. They made sure I got enough sleep, in fact there was no doubt I had to go to bed way too early sometimes. They never called attention to my speech and they never made me feel like I had a problem. I know my mom tried to have me eat good food, too. Well, good food is probably a matter of definition. There were several years when our diet was mostly eggs, deer meat, milk, potatoes and garden veggies. I remember I thought Mom's mush was great. It was a thick, goopy kind of food that filled our plate. We would smooth it down, put butter on it and then sprinkle it with cinnamon and sugar. Later I found out it was only milk thickened with flour. Well whatever it did for the diet I know not, but it did the trick for me and I thought it was good.

My speech problem slowly went away until it was only a memory. It was there, it was almost unbearable and then it was gone like the wind with no notice and no good-bye. I am thankful for what Mom and Dad did but I know that it was mostly God's grace and His miracle in my life that brought about total healing. It was an example of God working through natural situations in my life.

I am thankful for many things in my childhood. I had many friends, school was not difficult, my parents gave me much love and I enjoyed success in sports but the disappearance of my stuttering stands out as one of the most appreciated blessings.

Chapter Eleven

ANTIQUES-ANTIQUES-ANTIQUES

I must have walked past the drill press thousands of times when I was growing up and never did I think of it as a friend, an enemy or even an acquaintance. It was in the old shop and it simply was one of the "antique" tools/equipment that we had on our farm. During the time I was home on the farm the only new piece of equipment we got was a lawn mower. The truck was old, the combine was old, the "M" tractor was old and the buildings on our farm were even older. Most of our equipment was around a long time before I was born. Some of the antiques were:

The old anvil from our shop weighed almost one hundred pounds. It had round holes and square holes and it was used to make bale hooks, fix the sickle on the mower and I often used it to make toys. It had a point on one end which was used to round pieces of iron. On the other end it was flat with a round hole and a square hole. It certainly was a staple on the farm but it was an antique!

There was a vice in the old shop too. It would open really wide and was used maybe more than any other tool on the farm. I am sure Dave and I used it to make at least fifty wooden guns as well as many other items. Of course it was very handy, necessary even, in many farm projects, but it was actually an antique.

We had this cylinder-shaped sharpening stone that was about two inches thick and had a diameter of about twenty-four inches. To use it you sat on the seat and pushed the two pedals to make the cylinder go around. In that way you could sharpen an ax, a knife or pretty much anything that needed to be sharpened. A fun game I played by myself was to take my pocket knife, stand about twenty feet from a board, then hurl the knife and make it stick. I used the sharpening stone to keep my pocket knife nice and sharp.

You must have a swather to cut grain. We called it a windrower. Most farmers had gone to self-propelled machines but we still used a windrower that was pulled behind the tractor. The windrower would cut the grain with a long sickle and then the cut grain would ride a canvas to the side where it would come out in a windrow. We would allow the grain to dry for a few days and then come along with the combine to harvest it. Our windrower worked quite well but it was old and would often break down.

Most of the equipment on our farm was old but perhaps the oldest was our hay rake. All the surrounding farmers had what was called side deliverers. They had several large round cylinders with tines on. As you pulled it on the hay field the tines swept the hay into rows. Our equipment for putting hay into rows was our old antique rake that was used with horses at one time. Dad modified it so that we could pull it with a tractor. A person had to sit on the rake seat and when the tines were full of hay you stepped on a pedal and tripped the rake. If I had to consider only one piece of equipment on the farm an antique, it would be the rake, hands down!

We had an old one cylinder motor that was on the grain auger. An auger is used to take the grain from the truck and elevate it into the bin for storage. That motor had a perfect sound that I can still hear. I actually would like one today. I don't think I have heard another motor sound like ours and of course it was ancient.

We had an old manure spreader that worked well. We would load the manure from the barn into the spreader and then haul it out to the fields. There we would engage the bottom track. As the track brought the manure to the back it fell into a cylinder of tines that rotated. The rotating tines would fling the manure out onto the field. It seemed to me that everyone had a newer manure spreader than we had.

In the granary there were a couple of old benches with vises on them. When I was cleaning up the old pig barn foundation I hauled them out to the rock pile. I had never seen Dad use them and I thought I was doing a good deed by cleaning up old junk. Somehow Dad found out and he was really angry. He drove, too fast, down to the rock pile and retrieved them. They were placed back in the granary but I never did see them used.

Most of our field equipment was past its prime and outdated. The disc, the cultivator, the drag, the corn planter, the corn picker, the corn cultivator, the plows, the rock wagon and hay wagons all could have been featured on an antique show. Did they serve their purpose? They did but in their own small way.

We had this odd looking contraption that was a rope maker. It was a board shaped like a house with a peak on it. On the bottom of the board were three hooks in a triangle and the hooks would turn. There was a crank handle on the other side that would make the hooks swivel round and round. You would take three long strands of bale twine and tie each one to a hook. One person would stand with the rope maker in his hand and another person would stand holding the ends of the three lengths of twine. When the twine was twisted to the ends, you had a rope. Maybe it was not a fancy rope but it was one that was usable.

The forge in the old shop was a great tool that we used to heat up metal so we could bend it. You would start a fire with coal and then use the bellows to fan it. I think it was the kind of thing blacksmiths used. I remember Dad making bale hooks with the forge by heating up a metal rod and bending it. I cannot remember many things Dad made using the forge but I remember how fun it was to start the fire and get it extremely hot by cranking the bellows.

I could go on and on about the old things we had on the farm. If I had to single out one thing that I used the most it may be a tossup between the tools in the shop. If I had to narrow it down to one, I would say the huge drill press. I have no idea where Dad got it, maybe it belonged to his grandpa. I do not think I knew what it was called when I was growing up but I knew what it was used for. I would make all sorts of things with it. It was perfect for making the trigger guard on the wooden guns. I would trace a pattern on a piece of wood and then cut it out with a coping saw. When it was cut out, the gun would go over to the drill press and a hole for the trigger would be made. Presto, it was a gun. It also was used to drill the hole in my number one driver out of my golf bag. I could not have gotten that shaft in straight if it had not been for the drill press but then I also used it to accidently smash my thumb! Sometimes I would just drill different size holes for the fun of it. I also would take a piece of wood and drill tiny holes in it. Then I would stand the board on end and use it as a target for knife throwing. I would give myself a hundred points if the blade touched the hole. I became skilled enough with the knife that I bet I could have joined a circus. Well, maybe not.

There were toys on the farm too but those faded as I grew older and then the tools often were used as toys. The huge sand pile, not a sand box, grew into a weed patch, the pogo stick, that I could hop all the way to the barn on broke. The tether ball hung lifelessly near my basketball court and slowly the vise, the drill press, the sharpener that I could sit at and pedal and other tools became the toys of my childhood. Aside from the smashed thumb, the memories of tools long ago are today treasures in my heart.

Chapter Twelve

MY BIGGEST OUCH EVER

I have had many hurts in my day. Perhaps not as many as some but growing up on the farm where sticks, rocks, glass, nails and more seemed to be strewn everywhere, I may have experienced more than my quota.

I can remember every tiny detail of when the deer rifle kicked back and the scope made a half moon cut over my right eye. It is amazing that my eyebrow totally covers the scar today.

The day I fell head first from the rafters in the barn and landed on my head, I thought I was going to die. Dave and I were playing tag or some ludicrous game above the calf pens. There was no ceiling in the barn, only the rafters and then the roof joists. It seemed like we climbed up there often and would run from one end of the pens to the other. A person could jump from one beam to another and then across the aisle in the barn and be on the side where we milked the cows. One day as we ran across and over the beams I tripped on something and headed straight downward, as if I were doing a dive from the 5 meter diving board. It was one of the few times I was glad that our calf pens were not clean but rather had about six inches of manure in them. I landed head first with my legs spread-eagled in the air above me. I think it could have been very serious but all that happened was I totally lost my breath. I could not catch my breath and I thought I may die. Dave helped me into the house and slowly my breath came back and I was fine. A couple hours on the couch, some goodies from Mom and I was good to go.

Many times I would step on a nail or bang my head on something. Those hurts actually were not that bad. It seemed a little TLC from Mom and Epsom salt always did the trick in short order.

This was not an "ouch" time but I remember hurting so much when I was home with the mumps. I missed several days of school and even today looking at the pictures, it looks like I was a picture of warmed over death. One benefit of being sick in the winter was that I

53

got to sleep on the living room couch where it was nice and warm. In the winter, my bedroom would get below freezing, so of course when I was sick Mom allowed me to sleep downstairs.

There was the occasional stubbed toe, the sliver in the finger or just falling down when one was busy playing. I usually took those things in stride and went on my way in whatever I was doing. I had to play things kind of cool because if I was hurting it always was debatable if I should see Mom or Dad. Dad was the one who would most likely dismiss it and expect me to act like a man. Mom was the one who would be caring and also there with a frosted cracker or cookie. The one I went to depended on how much I hurt and how manly I felt!

The Ford tractor gave me as many "ouches" as all the nails, glass and boards combined. I usually was on the Ford in the fall when Dave and I plowed the stubble fields. The tractor Dave drove, the International M, pulled a three bottom plow. Our land was really rocky and many of them were underground and not visible. When Dave's plow hit a hidden rock the plow would come unhitched. Dave would stop, back up, hitch the plow again and slowly be on his way. That was far from what happened with the Ford. The Ford pulled a two bottom plow. The plow had to be attached to the drawbar on the back of the tractor with two pins. The way you controlled the plow was to raise or lower the drawbar with a lever on the right side of the tractor. If you wanted to unhitch the plow you had to take the two pins out and take the entire plow off. It seemed our land was better at growing rocks than wheat or oats! In the early summer we would spend days picking rocks but the next spring the field looked like the rocks had never been picked. When I was plowing with the Ford, if I hit a rock under the ground that was big enough, it would stop the tractor dead in its tracks. That often meant the tractor stopping and my body continuing to move towards the steering wheel. The way I sat on the tractor my nose lined up perfectly with the top of the steering wheel. The result was my nose would hit the steering wheel and my nose would lose, blood all over my shirt became a sign of fall plowing.

My biggest "ouch" by far came courtesy of the antique drill press in the shop. The drill press was about six feet tall and had a cylinder about the size of a football. There was a wheel on the top and a wheel on the bottom. We used it a lot as that was one easy way to drill holes for the guns we would make for cops and robbers. It just seemed that the drill press was used more than most tools on the farm. One day brother Ronald brought home some old golf clubs for me. There was a nine iron, a seven iron, a five iron, a driver, a few golf balls and some plastic practice balls. After several weeks I had a one hole golf course in which I teed off near the house and aimed for my putting surface. It was oiled sand and not grass, which was in the ditch near the mailbox. I stepped off the yardage and from tee to hole it was ninety yards, a nice nine iron for me. My problem was I did not have a putter. My other problem was I had this wooden driver that I would never use on a ninety yard hole. I got this great idea to make a putter out of the driver. I knew it would be easy because all I needed to do was to cut the shaft off and then put the shaft in the top of the wooden head of the driver. I would then have a putter that I could use by swinging it between my legs almost like Bob Pettit used to shoot his free throws for the St. Louis Hawks.

Finally, we had a rainy day so I did not have to work in the field. I decided this was the time to make my putter. I cut the shaft off with no problem so then it was only a matter of drilling the hole in the top of the wooden head. I knew that would be a bit difficult as the top of the driver was rounded and had a smooth slippery surface. All I needed to do was take my time and be careful. After I finished drilling the hole I would glue the shaft in the hole and I would have my putter. As I started the drill press, the bit slipped to the side, oh so slightly. I had the cylinder head of the drill press down to the club head which meant it was about three feet from the top of the drill. When I moved to straighten things out the cast iron cylinder slipped out of my hand and, like a NASA rocket, shot up to the top of the drill press shaft where my right thumb was resting. As the cylinder smashed my thumb into the top metal bracket I saw stars and more stars and then it felt like my thumb was going to explode. The pain shot through my body as if I had been shot. It felt like an eternity before I could move. Feeling faint and wobbly, I finally managed to get to the house. The only thing that could be done was to drill a hole in my thumb nail to relieve some of the built up pressure but that helped only a tiny bit. That night I tied my thumb to the bed post above my head to prevent the blood from going into the thumb. The pain was a little bit better the next day but it took a long time before it stopped hurting. About ten days later my thumb nail came off but by that time it was kind of a badge of courage and sign of manhood! My dad suffered several serious injuries on the farm and mine was not in the same league but still, I felt in a small way that it ushered me from boyhood to manhood. Many days later I finished the putter and it actually worked quite well but was it worth it? I would never want that pain again but then how can a person play golf without a putter?

Chapter Thirteen

DOWN SOUTH

Down south often means in one of the southern states. If you talk to snow birds they may say that they like to winter down south. When I meet a new person they may talk in such a way that I think they grew up down south, maybe in Texas or Mississippi or Alabama.

When I grew up on the farm we had an entirely different meaning for the term "down south". If Dad told us we should pick rocks down south he did not mean in Mississippi but rather he meant on the land we farmed that belonged to Uncle Jim. Uncle Jim had eighty acres of land. Most of the time land was divided into sections or quarters. A quarter was a section divided into fourths. Jim owned half of a quarter. His land was divided into three parcels. One parcel was summer fallowed each year, one was planted into crop and one was native prairie land that had never been broken up.

To get there we drove south a half mile, took a right turn over the bridge and then a quick left to head south again. We would then be driving on a dirt path that was worn into a road parallel to Rollof's pasture. When we came to the south end of Rollof's pasture, we were driving on Uncle Jim's native prairie land that had never seen a plow. East and south of the prairie was crop land. Each year one half of it would be summer fallowed, meaning it was not planted but rather kept black. That was meant to give the soil a rest. The remaining parcel would be planted into crops. I am not sure what kind of business deal Dad had with Uncle Jim but I remember it must have been kind of a gentlemen's contract. When we were taking grain to town, right away I remember Dad would say something like this load goes to Jim. Jim never worked with us on his land but there were times he came during harvest just to chat and see what kind of crop he or we had. I remember he would come down and stay for an hour or so. Sometimes he would take a hand full of grain, and if it was wheat he would carefully blow out the chaff and then put some in his mouth, as if it were gum.

The prairie hay was like no other hay, certainly very different than alfalfa. I have no idea what food value it had for the cows but it was slippery and had what we called prairie needles in it. These needles would stick to your clothes but they did not hurt like a needle used to give shots! There was also June grass in the prairie hay and every summer a man would come with some antique machines that were used to harvest June grass. He would drop them off and then pick up the machines and the June grass seed in a week or two. Dad would just drive around the prairie with those machines and they would fill up with the seeds of the plants. June grass is a main component in lawn seed used primarily in Europe and central United States. I imagine the seeds from "down south" made some homeowner in an expensive house happy. Our stacks made with the prairie hay always had a unique look because about them. The hay stack often had the look of a rounded pyramid because when the stack was made you could not stand near the edge. For that reason, as the stack got higher, the edges came in towards the middle! Alfalfa hay was always dusty and dirty while prairie hay was shiny and prickly.

For some reason prairie hay seemed to keep our water jug cooler than other hay. Our high tech water jug was a glass gallon jug wrapped in a burlap sack. In the morning we would run the water until it was as cold as it would get and then wet down the burlap sack that was around the water jug. If we set the jug in the shade, under the hay, it would stay cool much of the day. Maybe not as cool as a fancy electric water cooler but we thought it did the job well.

The crop land was used differently from year to year. Oats, wheat, and barley were rotated on the fields. I remember years when we had really good crops "down south" and I remember some years that it was hardly worth the gas to harvest it. In a normal year, when we would start out combining, we could go around the field once or maybe another half round before we had to empty the fifty bushel tank. I remember one very dry year we had to make several rounds before we got a tank full of grain. When I think back on those years, it reinforces the idea that I was not a good farmer because I liked it when harvest went quickly. It meant that there was less time spent in the itchy dust generated by the combine. Little did I think about the fact that a scant harvest meant less money for the coming year.

Working "down south" was always better than working near the farm. It meant that I could drive the mile or so there in high gear on the tractor. It meant that there were fewer rocks to pick as compared to the land to the west or east of our farm. That land seemed to grow more rocks than crops!

There was a grove of trees in the middle of Uncle Jim's crop land. That grove provided shade for sitting while we ate lunch and the leaves of the trees also were important if you needed to go to the bathroom. Of course there were no port-a-potties in those days!

One fall Dave and I were plowing down south. For some reason we were plowing the long way, which was north and south and not the shorter east/west direction. I imagine that was a year that the south parcel of land was in crops. Dave and I had no grand ideas of ever farming so our work habits were not the best some times. One rule we had was when the sun set, the day's work was done. There could be exceptions, but not often. We would watch the sun and the second it went down we were on our way home. If we were on the south end of the field, the plow came out of the ground and we headed home like the horse that is nearing his barn after a long ride. One time Dad asked us why we didn't plow to the north end and then head home. I thought that was a poor idea! We were in a hurry to get home. It meant a bike trip up to the lake with washcloth and soap to wash the day's dust off. I could almost smell that mush with cream and cinnamon on or those hard boiled eggs with mustard mixed in for supper. Really, after a day on the tractor, one gets dirty and hungry!

When Uncle Jim died Dad no longer farmed his land. I never asked Dad if Jim offered to sell it and he didn't have the money or if he just did not want to continue farming that much land. It is a shame that the native prairie land did not remain that way but black dirt is money in a farmer's pocket so the land was broken up after it was sold.

"Down South", I still think of the farm land when someone I meet talks about the south!

Chapter Fourteen

BIG BIKE-LITTLE BIKE

We had many forms of transportation on our farm. We had the Ford tractor which was easy to drive and was used for much of the field work. We had the "M" International which we used to do the heavier kind of work on the farm. There was "Big Red" which was our 1935 farm truck. It was a grand vehicle. With a front windshield that cranked out, a double clutch stick on the floor and wide fenders, it was a classic. Oh, we had a car too. It was a 1953 Ford with a flat-8 engine. I learned to drive it when I was 12 but had to wait until I was fourteen to get my driver's license.

When you grow up on a farm you learn to drive many vehicles and do it at a young age. However my real mode of transportation was the little bike. I would say we were not very creative. We had two bikes on the farm. One was much smaller than the other so of course they became the "little bike" and the "big bike". The little bike took me to real places. I tended to pretend and dream a lot so I went to places around the world and explored far off sights. My little bike took me to places like Grandma's house, Rollof's farm, Aunt Bertie's farm, my friend Ricky's place and to Lake Tewaukon. Those places were real and the things I received there were tangible. I rode to Aunt Bertie's and Uncle Obert's to earn money. I rode to Grandma Lee's for garden goodies, cookies and hugs. I rode to Ricky's to play ball. I rode to Lake Tewaukon to swim, water ski, pick choke cherries and wash the harvest dust and dirt off so I could sleep at night.

I felt the little bike gave me independence. I could ask Mom if I could go to Grandma's house and if she said yes I did not need to get a ride. Grandma and Grandpa Lee lived three miles away and that was an easy ride on my bike. I felt so grownup when I could go by myself. Of course the rewards of being there were an added bonus. Grandma had fruit trees, several kinds of berries like strawberries, blueberries, currents, gooseberries, huckleberries, plums and more. When the berries had been eaten there were always cookies and then before I would leave there was always a big hug.

My little bike took me the half mile to Rollof and Hazel's farm. There I would haul bales for a day and sometimes take home as much as twenty dollars. They would also feed me great dinners and lunches. I would also bike to Uncle Obert and Aunt Bertie's. There I would help with the hay and, of course, enjoy fried chicken for dinner and cookies and bars for lunch.

The most fun place to bike was Lake Tewaukon. The lake was a half mile north of our farm. I would pride myself in riding from our house to the lake shore without touching the handlebars. The lake was many things to me and the little bike would get me there for them all. My brother Ronald and also sister Janet's husband, John, had boats. and that was what we used to water ski. I got so I could take off on one ski or use two and then come around and drop one off. I thought I was pretty cool in my blue, sharp swim trunks going around Lake Tewaukon on one ski!

Actually the most often use for the lake was a bath! We did not have indoor bathroom facilities at home so in the summer the lake was our bathtub. Each night, before I went to bed, I would bike to the lake with soap and towel in hand. After swimming for a bit, I would soap up and then swim some more. In the late summer I had to swim out from shore a bit as there would usually be green slippery scum near the shore. That would only happen when the wind was from the west, which was most of the time. Sometimes I would stop at the east end of the lake and catch some fireflies to bring home. I would carry the jar into the house, turn the lights off without asking Mom, and then show her the fireflies in the dark room. When I was finished admiring them I would always let them go.

These many things were mostly possible because I had our little red bike. It was a "meat and potatoes" kind of bike. No multispeed, no fancy handlebars, and no speedometer to see how fast or how far I rode. It had a red and white plastic seat, front and rear chrome fenders, a kickstand and you had to back pedal to brake. I could ride far and fast, in my mind anyway. Occasionally there would be a flat tire but Dave and I became experts at fixing the holes in the tubes. We really did not have a choice because there was no money for new tubes and if we were to wait for Dad, we may have to go several days without our transportation.

One time I decided to imitate my town friends by putting baseball cards in the spokes but that just did not seem to be right. I decided it looked stupid, it damaged the cards and it seemed to create wind resistance. Besides, who wants Mickey Mantle and Hank Aaron going round and round until they are dizzy?

The big bike was similar to the little bike except I did not ride it very much. Dave was older than I, so he rode that one. It also was a "meat and potatoes" kind of bike, with no frills. It had straight handlebars, fenders in front and back but it was black. When I did graduate to it, I could go faster because the tires were twenty-six inches, while the little bike had twenty-four inch tires.

I grew to love the little bike. It expanded my world. It often took me out of my imaginary world and put me in the real world which I think was good. It actually gave me options. I could sit on the barn roof and dream about faraway places or I could get on my bike and go to real places. I loved having different choices of ways to spend my time and that became an important part of my childhood.

Our famous out-house many years after its prime

Chapter Fifteen

THE PREEMINENT THRONE

I would be remiss if I did not write this chapter. The preeminent throne is, of course, a bathroom, but if I want to be accurate it was really our outhouse. Most people have experienced outhouses in some form and some place. At camp grounds, I have seen many. Some are acceptable, some are fantastic and others, a person is almost afraid to use.

In rural North Dakota, in the fifties and sixties when I grew up, there were many shapes and forms of preeminent thrones, bathrooms or out-houses. I had favorite ones and I had ones that I did not like, but for sure, our preeminent throne on the farm was one of a kind, unique and interesting!

Aunt Bertie and Uncle Obert lived a mile from us. They lived a life style in great contrast to ours. Their farm was modern, progressive and an example to those who lived near them. Bertie's house was warm, updated and cozy. Their bathroom, I will not call it a throne, was a model to be desired and copied. When you came into her kitchen the bathroom was to the right. I realize that having a bathroom next to the kitchen is not ideal, but that was often the case back then. You could walk through the bathroom and be in the master bedroom. Obert had installed modern plumbing so they had a flush toilet, a cast iron tub and a nice vanity. I would say, it was worth a trip to Bertie and Obert's, just to use their bathroom. Mom never mentioned it, but she must have had thoughts each time we visited. Bertie's home was so much more modern than ours. I would say her bathroom was number one in decor and function!

Grandpa Sampson, well, his toilet was Spartan like. It sat in the middle of an almost empty basement, with no walls or stall! But it flushed and gushed and that was important! I liked it, but I was on high alert when I used it. If there was the slightest indication that Mom may be coming downstairs to make sure we were good, I was finished with my business in a second!

Grandma and Grandpa Lee had an outhouse but they also had a pail upstairs. Their upstairs was a long room with a bedroom on each end with two curtains separating the bedrooms. The curtains were used to hide the pail and give a minimal amount of privacy. When I was little, I did not like to use their bathroom. The room was kind of dark and the curtains made the bathroom even darker. I always felt that there may be something coming out of the shadows to scare me.

Wood Lake School had two outhouses. Boys would go out the front door, turn to their right and straight back was a one-hole outhouse. Girls would go out the front door, turn to their left, and walk past the south windows as they went to their destination. It seemed to me that the outhouses were the same, except for the wording on the front. The worst thing about Wood Lake's outhouses was they were used year round, which meant it was a cold trek in January!

The preeminent throne in Sargent County had to be the three-holer on our farm. It was nestled back into the trees, north of our house. It was not really very attractive but it was partially hidden in the grove. It was large and as you entered it, there was a choice of THREE seats. The two on the right were adult sized and the one on the left was about six inches lower. There was ample room for papers, magazines and catalogs. We usually had Penneys, Sears and Montgomery Wards stocked for reading, looking and also okay toilet paper! The yellow pages always went first. Of course, the peach wrappings in the fall were the best toilet paper. There was a cupula on top but it really was not needed because there was plenty of ventilation through the walls! Did Dad use any chemicals for the waste? Absolutely not as that would cost money! There was door that could be locked with an eye hook, but you really did not need that because as you entered, you just flipped the "busy" sign down.

The location was perfect. If you were pretty sure there would be no company coming, you could leave the door open and admire Mom's flowers. It was nestled in the trees so there would often be birds to listen to. A couple of long steps to the north was the creek bank, and for several weeks in the spring, you could hear the water rushing over the rock dam. An important item was the "busy" sign. It protruded out from the front about 12 inches and could easily be seen from the house.

The biggest reason our outhouse was the preeminent throne was all of the business that was conducted inside. Dave and I could sit for a long time discussing our problems, our plans for the day, our teenage difficulties and more. We could also make plans for a new kind of wooden gun, how we may be able to avoid work that day or the next, and as we got older there were plenty of discussions about Mom, Dad and girls. All of which we felt presented big time problems at times! So, I guess I would say that the business conducted in the preeminent throne was less important than the discussions and plans that took place.

We did have a pail in the house for the winter time. It was upstairs in a box-like compartment right in the middle of the hallway. Sometimes I wonder if we suffered in the winter because there was no place, with décor and ambiance, to solve our problems!

Mom and Dad put a bathroom in after I left for college. I am sure Mom was so pleased but I kind of felt bad for the preeminent throne as it sat in the grove of trees, useless and unwanted. I guess there are times we can say good-bye and welcome modern conveniences.

Chapter Sixteen

GLENWOOD

Glenwood is a town between St. Paul, Minnesota and Geneseo, North Dakota. Whenever I now drive on I-94 I see there is a sign as you near Alexandria. It says Glenwood is south about fifteen miles. I have not been to Glenwood in my adult life. I can see on the map that it is on a lake as are many towns in Minnesota. However in the late fifties Glenwood was a special place. It was a destination that I loved. There was no I-94 but Glenwood was on Highway 55 and could be seen as a person drove towards the Twin Cities.

There were no family vacations when I was growing up. Dad, only Dad, went on Farmers Union trips several times. A bus load of farmers would go to Washington D. C. to talk about farm problems but Dad also went to sightsee and take pictures. When he came home we could count on seeing "trip slides" again and again and again. I don't know if women went on those bus trips but I know Mom never went. There were several times we went to the Minnesota State Fair and Mom never went on those fun jaunts either. Dad traveled several times for health reasons and one time Ronald had to go out state for surgery, but of course, those would not be considered family vacations. Joan and Helen, in the mid-eighties, were able to accompany Mom to California where two of her brothers lived. I think they had a grand time as women in that situation would! Helen said they went with Mom to buy a new outfit before they went. Mom bought a pair of pants which was the first time she had ever owned a pair of pants! It was also the first time Mom had been in an airplane. As far as I know that was "the vacation" in Mom's life. But for me, when I was growing up, there were no family vacations of any kind.

One thing we did as a family was to drive to Glenwood, Minnesota in the summer to be with Mom's relatives. I do not remember if we went every year for a while or if we went a few times over several years. I remember them well, whatever the timing was, and they always seemed to be fun. Mom had brothers in the Twin Cities. Mom's brother Olaf, and his wife Mable, lived in Minneapolis on Harriet Avenue. Olaf was one of my favorite uncles. It seemed like he enjoyed life and was always happy. He would joke a lot and was just fun to be around. He and Mable never had a family. Philip, another brother of mom's, and his wife May lived in New Brighten just north of the fairgrounds in St. Paul. We would stay with them when we went to the Minnesota State Fair. They had two children, Philip Junior and Jolene. They were a lot older than I because Mom was the youngest child, by ten years, in a family of thirteen children. Most of our cousins on Mom's side were almost old enough to be from an older generation.

Glenwood was about half way between the Twin Cities of Minneapolis and St. Paul and our farm, so that was a good place to meet. Our reunion of sorts, would happen on a Sunday and it consisted of a picnic, conversation and usually a ball game with the cousins. Of course the conversation was not something I was into as a kid, but the ball game was a big thing and the food was even better. It seemed that the city folks always brought food that was extra special. The day always seemed to be long because we would leave early in the morning and get home well after dark. Mom would always want to stay as long as possible, as she did not get to see Olaf and Philip very often. Our family always spent a lot more time with Dad's relatives than with Mom's. Part of that was we lived closer to Dad's relatives but I think the real reason was Dad was not into Mom's family in a big way. I remember Olaf and Mable visiting one time on the farm but I do not remember Philip and May ever coming to visit us when I was little.

It was a big deal for me when I found out that we would be going to Glenwood on a particular Sunday. It seemed like a lengthy ride but now as I look back it really was a fairly short drive. We would go south to Sisseton, then to Brown's Valley and take highway 7 straight east to Glenwood. It seemed like it was two hundred miles or more but today, if one googles it, the mileage is one hundred and three miles. Dad would always have to check the car before we went. It seemed like he often did that early Sunday morning. There were times he changed the oil and for sure he had to "put on gas" before we left but we still were usually on the road by 8:00 AM. Dad never put "in gas" but always on and I never did figure out how a car could run with gas on it! Off we would go early in the morning. Mom was always excited as this was the one day of the year that was geared towards her family. Dave would sit behind Mom and I would sit behind Dad. Helen sat in front between Mom and Dad, while Joan sat in the back between Dave and me. To make the ride seem interesting we would play games. One game was to see who could count the most horses on their side of the road. There must have been a lot of horses because that occupied us much of the time. I think some of the time was spent asking if we were almost there and of course teasing Helen and Joan.

Another favorite thing we would do is look for Burma Shave signs and read them as we passed. Burma Shave would put a saying on signs with about five or six signs for each saying. Some of the sayings were: *"said Farmer Brown, who's bald, on top, wish I could rotate, the crop". "Passing cars, when you can't see, may get you, a glimpse, of eternity." "If daisies are your, favorite flower, keep pushing up those, miles-per-hour"*. Someone in the front seat would spot a sign coming up and horses would be forgotten as we strained to see the slogan. There must have been a dozen or more Burma Shave signs on the way, but of course on the way home it was usually dark so that game was out the window.

When we arrived in Glenwood it was a BIG hello to all of the family. Mom would hug her brothers and the men would kind of stiffly reach out their hand to say "hello, it is good to see you" although the words did not accompany the muted greeting. You know that those Norwegian men can't be too expressive. The day would come to an end all too quickly. I remember one of the best things. There was food available all day long. There was a dinner and then supper but there was food on the table all day long. I may have eaten enough to store some up for the coming week! There was usually a ball game with the young boys and adult men. I remember hitting the softball into the lake one time but my brother Ronald was able to wade in and get it. Was it a home run? Yes, all the way!

Glenwood, it holds a special place in my memory. Someday I will have to revisit the park in town by the lake to see what it looks like in real adult life.

Chapter Seventeen

I AM CHAMPION

I kind of lived in my own little world in rural North Dakota. Our farm was about ten miles southwest of Geneseo and ten miles southeast of Cayuga. Veblen was maybe twelve miles but it was south of our farm, actually in South Dakota. We seldom went there unless it was to visit Grandpa Sampson and Uncle Jim. When I was a sophomore in high school we started attending church in town and then we went to Veblen more often. But really my world consisted very little of the "outside world". My brother and I mostly spent our time in the field doing field work or when we were lucky enough to not hear Dad tell us what to do that day we would play ball, make things or ride our bikes. We had two bikes, the little bike and the big bike. Of course, way back then they were one speed cruisers which were really fun to ride. We often helped Mom in the garden, mowed the lawn and did other work around the yard as well. It seemed like in the summer there was always a plea from Mom to weed the garden, mow the grass, and clean the chicken house or some other chore that was mundane. However there was nothing mundane about cleaning the chicken house as the ammonia was the worst smell in the world. Even with the evening summer chores, there were a couple of summers Dad allowed me to play Little League baseball and that was something I could have done every day as I loved to play ball.

I was very surprised and afraid when Dad told Dave and me that George Bracken in Lidgerwood had a Golden Glove boxing program and he signed us up for it. I could not believe Dad signed us up for boxing, but I did remember Dad telling stories of his boxing when he was a young man. I don't know if he liked it or not but I was told that he was good.

Off we went the next evening to Lidgerwood. I did not know what to expect but Dad told us to take our swim suits, t-shirts and shoes. I remember I asking which shoes to take as I had my church shoes that Mom would polish often on Saturday night, my work shoes that I almost never wore because I went barefoot all summer and then I had these cheesy looking low cut Converse tennis shoes that had arrived in Aunt Ragna's huge box of used clothing from California. In that last box there was really nothing for me, but way in the bottom were these old black tennis shoes that had a small hole in one toe. They fit me and Mom said I should keep them. Aunt Ragna's clothes boxes are another story. Anyway, I could not really figure out what I would need my swim suit for if we were going boxing, but I took it because Dad said I should.

We arrived in Lidgerwood about 6:30 and Dad said the boxing lessons started at 7:00 in the Lidgerwood High School gym. That made me feel a bit more comfortable as my brother Ronald had gone to school there and I had been in the gym many times. We arrived early and walked into the gym with our old duffle bags stuffed with clothes. There was a basketball hoop on each end of the gym and then on the west end there was a stage the length of the gym and about four feet high. I remembered Ronald and Janet doing different school activities on the stage. An older gentleman approached us, held out his hand and said, "Hi, my name is George, I am glad you came". I wanted to say "Hi, my name is Carmen and I am not glad I came" Of course I did not because I would never have talked to an adult like that and also in those situations I often could not get my words out. George talked to Dad for a while and I got the idea that Dad had told him about Dave and me. It sounded like George was expecting us to be kind of good.

After a couple of minutes George said good-bye to Dad and told us to come on stage so we could weigh in. He pointed to some marked spaces on the floor and said we could leave our clothes there and get on the scale. Leave our clothes, I was horrified! I did not come here to get naked. I did not even like to get naked in front of Dave or Ronald or Dad and here I was told to get naked in front of about 30 boys. I cautiously looked around and sure enough there were naked guys standing everywhere. I looked at the gym door and hoped that there was a sign on the outside to keep girls out. I hurried as fast as I could to get my clothes off, step on the scale, and then get into my swim suit and t shirt. I saw that nobody else had a swim suit on. Everyone else had different kind of shorts that looked a lot better than my swimsuit.

When I was in the fourth grade, I did not have a nice swim suit like I did in high school. That one was a stretchy one that fit well. It was blue with a white band on the top and I thought I looked pretty cool in it but now, in the fourth grade, I longed for shorts like the others. I mean real shorts, not some old hand me down swim suit that set me apart from everyone else.

I remember going to Lidgerwood weekly for several months. We were divided into weight classes and it dawned on me that was why we needed to weigh in with no clothes on. I was big for my age so even though I was in the fourth grade, I was boxing against boys in the fifth or sixth grade. Actually, my boxing skills came in handy a couple of years later but again, that is another story. The winter passed quickly with weekly boxing lessons which I actually enjoyed. Dave and I more than held our own. It started to be kind of fun. We had these big gloves. They were about as big as my head it seemed. I think that was so we could not hurt others, if we happened to hit someone. George taught us the finer points of boxing. *Keep your right toe pointed forward, keep your shoulders straight, keep your head up and when you punch, lead with your left hand and then come in with your right hand.*

Sometime in late spring, the lessons came to an end and to finish it out we would have a tournament. I really don't remember a lot of that but I know I was good enough to win my weight class and be called the CHAMPION. I did bring home a gold boxing glove pin about the size of a nickel. I thought to myself that it was worth it to get all naked one time. I was so proud and when we arrived home I raced into the house to show Mom. She admired it and said I must have been very good but I knew that she did not agree with Dad about the boxing lessons. The next day for school I did not know what I should do but I had to bring my boxing pin to show my teacher. I thought that I couldn't just walk up to her and show her, as that might look like I was bragging. I had my plan in place as I got on the bus. When I got to school I would bring my gold boxing medal to the teacher and ask her to save it for me so that I would not lose it. It worked! I am sure she knew what I was doing but she was nice enough to just admire it, compliment me and then tell me she would be glad to save it for me until the end of the school day. Now, fifty-five years later, of course,

I have no idea what happened to the gold pin. I do remember saving it for a long time and thinking it was a big deal. It was so valuable to me I even kind of forgot how terrible it was standing naked in front of all those guys! Memories, they tend to keep us in touch with the past and give us hope for the future. Pins, medals and ribbons tend to be retired into boxes, sometimes special boxes, and collect dust for another generation.

Chapter Eighteen

BENNY

I always wanted a horse when I was growing up. I remember the day Dad sold our last horse. It was kind of a golden color and was not broken to ride yet. I loved that horse and never understand why we could not keep him. Dad had a million horse stories. In his stories he would ride them, he would break them and he would work with them. I read every Black Stallion book at least twice and maybe many more times. I read the book, Black Beauty, and every other horse book I could find. The year I handed in one hundred and ten book reports in school, I think at least half of them were about horses. I even tried for hours on end to draw pictures of horses. Even though my desire and dream of owning a horse never became reality, Benny was the next thing to a horse.

Benny was a Saint Bernard dog, a huge dog. He was just a tiny ball of fur when we got him and his siblings came into the farming area too. Uncle Halvor got a puppy, George Lee got a puppy and neighbor Roloff got a puppy. Someone must have been giving them away and wanted to do a "take all" kind of deal! Perhaps my dad "took all" and then peddled them off to friends and neighbors. I remember he was by far the largest, softest and most interesting dog we ever had.

After Benny went to dog heaven, in not such a nice way I am certain, we had other dogs. In fact, we always had a dog on the farm. I don't know where we would get them but we would get a puppy and I came to love every dog we had. One puppy on our farm, was a brown and white little one who just wanted to be with us all the time. Dave and I were helping Dad and move a big heavy pipe. You know these farm boys were strong! One of us, I think it was I, dropped their end of the pipe which landed right on top of our little puppy. It injured him so bad that Dad had to put him to sleep. That was a sad day.

We also had Tiny. Tiny was a cocker spaniel with wavy, golden hair who loved to ride in the truck with us. He wanted to go with us wherever we went. Of course we would never allow a dog to come in the car or in the house either, so Tiny often had to spend time alone. In the winter he would spend time in the warm barn but would always come out to play with us when we went skating or sledding or just romping in the snow. One day, while riding with us in the 35 Ford truck he leaned out too far and went head long into the ditch. Dave was driving the truck, he screeched to a halt and I ran back to save Tiny. Tiny simply stood up, shook himself and ran back to jump in the truck again. Of course, as Dave floored the truck and we sped away there was Tiny, with his head and half of his body out the window, but this time I was hanging on.

After Benny we never had a big dog again. I suspect it may have been because Benny probably ate more than anyone in the family. I don't even dare think about who had to clean up after him when he went to the bathroom as he was not smart enough to use the three-holer. Dad tried to make a bird dog out of him but that was a disaster. Benny would take off when he smelled a bird and try to catch it. Not really what a bird dog is supposed to do but Benny did not mind.

Maybe it was because I wanted a horse so badly but I remember trying to ride Benny. I am not sure I was successful, but I do know he was up to the challenge. I probably fell off because there was no dog saddle! Benny would follow us around all the time but as he matured, he started to get into mischief. Farm dogs are free to roam anyplace they desire but there are limits. You just can't tie a dog up or put him on a leash when you live in the country. Benny got this idea that maybe he could curb his appetite a bit if he could catch some chickens! That was not a good idea. I cannot remember how we solved that problem but I remember Dad saying that once a dog started doing that it was only a matter of time until he had to be put down.

Then the BIG trouble started. Benny was supposedly sleeping in the barn at night. I am not sure how we arranged that as the door would have had to be wide open for him to get in, but anyway, that was the plan. One night we heard the cattle being very restless, making noise outside the barn. Dad said he would go out and see what was happening. He turned off the yard light and then told Mom to wait a few minutes before she turned it on. The idea was for Dad to get out in the dark and then have the light turned on to see if he could spot any wild animal with the cows. In about ten minutes Mom turned the yard light on and we heard Dad yelling like, well yelling like Dad usually did not yell. He came into the house and said several dogs had herded our cattle against the barn and were harassing them.

That was the beginning of the end of the Saint Bernard era on the area farms. A couple more times the cattle were harassed but in the end all of the Saint Bernards on the neighborhood farms disappeared from the landscape! No more Benny, no more trying to ride this giant dog and no more romping in the snow with him. He could lick, push me over and clean my face better than Tiny but on the farm you cannot have cattle chasers. . I remember one day Dad said he was going hunting and would take Benny with him. Later Dad came back with two pheasants and his shotgun but no Benny. Dad never mentioned Benny again.

Chapter Nineteen

CHICKEN POOP

Chicken Poop has to be the worst thing in the world! The looks are bad, the feel of it between your toes is awful but the worst is the smell. When I was growing up I could endure most anything. There were times when I had to wade ankle deep in cow manure to do some work and that was not too bad. There were times I would step on a nail and Mom had to pull it out, that was not too big a deal. But, when Mom or Dad gave the dreaded orders to clean the chicken house I wanted to run away and never return. I thought if this is what farming is all about I will never live on a farm. I will get a job in the cities so I will never have to clean chicken poop again

Chickens were a part of the farm food chain and farm economy. They provided food and money for our family. We had these wonderful wooden egg crates that we used. The wooden box was square and you could put three dozen eggs in each layer. We would then put five layers of eggs so that the top of the eggs could be seen just peeping over the edge. When we had a full crate we would take them into Cayuga and sell them. There was a business man, Benny Flash, who would buy them and then sell them to area stores. I remember that a person had to be very careful so that there were no big bumps when we drove to town. When we arrived at Benny's, he would come out to carry the egg crate into his store. I always thought it was fun to go with Dad to sell eggs. Benny seemed like such a jolly, likeable guy but I did think he looked kind of funny. He was more than a bit overweight and he had a big double chin that jiggled when he talked. He also swayed back and forth when he walked, especially when he was carrying the crate of eggs.

Chickens were also a big part of our food chain on the farm. I am certain I ate more eggs than any boy in the world. Of course, Mom would use them all the time for baking but we would often enjoy a meal of eggs. On Sunday, after we came home from church, Mom would frequently make fried egg sandwiches with a side of dill pickles as a special treat. Our eggs were large so Mom would break the yolk when she fried them and then put one hard egg between two delicious pieces of homemade bread. They were extra good if we had mayo to put on the bread. We did not have mayo all the time because that was something we had to buy and when money was short the mayo was one of the first items to be cut. Eggs actually made me a great cook. If Mom was gone, when I came in from the field, I would make five or six hard boiled eggs. I enjoyed mashed eggs with a generous dollop of mustard. If I had enough energy, I would have a fancy meal by toasting two slices of Mom's delicious homemade bread to compliment my eggs.

The eggs were great, but, the chickens were not my favorite farm animals. We had free roaming chickens, which meant they had the run of the farm. I would often be running or walking around the yard and *squish*, there was chicken poop between my toes or on the bottom of my foot. I sometimes thought that the chickens did not like me because they seemed to have a sense of where to relieve themselves so the poop would be right in my path. At a young age I decided it was not worth the effort to look out for the poop because it was everywhere. The best I could do was wipe the bottoms of my feet in the grass or take a small twig and try to wedge it from between my toes. I would then walk to the barn and wash my feet in the water tank. Of course, the water tank was for the cows, not for people.

Chickens were a good thing on our farm but sometimes it was difficult to admit that. The worst was the odor when I went into the chicken house. The chicken house was small, maybe fifteen feet by fifteen feet. The door was on the southwest corner. As I went in, there was a bank of nests on the west wall. There were two tiers, kind of like a first floor and a second floor condo! On the north wall was a series of boards stretching from east to west and that was where the chickens roosted at night and relieved themselves often. On the east wall was a water trough and a large wooden box, kind of like the container in which you would find paper towels to dry your hands in a public bathroom. These kinds of containers had the towels come out the bottom. This large container was where we dumped the oyster shells for the chickens. I was told we needed to feed that to the chickens so the egg shells would be hard enough.

Under the roosting place is where the odor emanated, and that was the most undesirable place on the farm. The nitrogen, in the poop, started its decomposing process here and in the end gave off that awful ammonia stench. That space was about twenty-five percent of the floor but it contained ninety percent of the poop and odor. The difficult part was that I had to stoop over and walk part way under the roost to get at the poop. Before I did that, I made sure I cleaned the boards off above the floor, because if I didn't I would come out with poop on my back. I was usually shoeless in the summer but not when I cleaned the chicken poop! I would take a pitchfork and pull the poop out from under the roost. It would then be pitched out the door and onto a pile south of the building. I have to admit I didn't always remove that pile of poop in a timely manner. There were summers when most of the time there was a temple of poop just outside the door. I really do not think I was lazy, but to handle the poop was awful. If it remained piled there for some time the odor would fade a bit and then I could pitch it into the manure spreader and take it out to the field. I have been told that chicken poop is an excellent fertilizer; just do not use it on your garden!

Joan and Dave avoiding the chicken poop
Our dilapidated granary is in the background

To be honest, I was never cut out to be a farmer. However, growing up, the chicken poop did not enhance my attitude towards farm life. As I grew into adulthood I sometimes heard the term, "chicken sh**" and I think I know from where it came. It never was used in a positive or complementary way!

Chapter Twenty

MINNESOTA STATE FAIR

We sat on the dry harvest straw while eating our afternoon lunch. Most of the time we would sit for a half hour or so but not this day. The stubble field was slowly becoming a field of straw and dirt which would wait for the winter snow to accumulate and leave precious moisture for crops in the spring. Fall plowing was always a mixed bag. It was a mixture of straw, large rocks, and deadlines that pointed towards school. With a tiny two bottom plow behind the Ford and a three bottom plow behind the "M", the days seemed to stretch into weeks as we drove up and down the furrows with only minimal stubble turned to dirt. I would follow the furrow with the front wheel of the Ford Tractor going straight towards the end of the field but behind me was only this tiny implement. With each trip across the field, the plow would convert thirty-six inches of straw to a black and yellow field. Dave would drive the International "M", with the narrow front wheels. He would have to pay more attention to keep the furrow straight but he probably did a better job than I. The "M" could pull a three bottom plow so that was four and a half feet. Turning over seven feet of straw with each journey across the field meant plowing a thirty acre field was a timely chore.

Our fields of thirty acres were a quarter mile long and as wide as three football fields. Going back and forth, turning seven feet of stubble each time, translated into many hours of work. This day it seemed to stretch on forever, as we knew our rule of work had to be broken. Our rule was "sun down" and home. Well, we had to finish this day because Dad had promised us a trip to the Minnesota State Fair in St. Paul if we finished plowing. We had to finish plowing, drive to St. Paul and get back for the start of school after Labor Day. As I watched the brilliant orange sun hide its face behind the western horizon, I glanced across the field. My guess was, we would be working well into the night. I did not enjoy being a prophet but, that I was. Daylight slowly disappeared, and with the darkness came the tractor headlights that could not even find the end of the field but would shine enough for us to see our furrow. Finally, success, Dave and I lifted up the plows and headed home just before midnight. The straw covered field had been transformed into a massive field of black dirt, rocks and bits of straw peeking out from big ugly clumps, we had finished. As we climbed into bed, we knew that tomorrow would be a new day with travel, excitement and fun!

Early the next morning we headed east towards St. Paul. As usual, Dad had to take time at the last minute to change oil on the car and gas had to be put "on" the car. Never did figure out how that darn old Ford car could go with gas on it instead of in it. There was no freeway yet, so we would head east on highway 11 and then catch highway 10 into the cities. This time we were staying with Uncle Phil and Aunt May and that was why Dad drove highway 10. They lived a short distance from the fairgrounds, which was on the north side of the cities. When we stayed with Uncle Olaf and Aunt Mable, we would take highway 55 into the west side of Minneapolis. Uncle Olaf and Aunt Mable were my favorites to stay with but the big perk staying with Uncle Phil and Aunt May was they may take us out to eat. The last time we had stayed with them they took us to a pancake house and we could eat different kinds of syrup and have as many pancakes as we could eat. That was fun for all of us, the variety for me and the treat they gave us was special.

As we neared St. Cloud, I pretended that I was busy reading a book because I knew what would happen. Highway 10 took us past the prison and Dad would always comment that if we were not good that is the place we would be sent. I really did not like it when he would say that. The entire structure looked wicked to me. It had these tall stone walls with barb wire above them and then these little houses on each corner. Dad said men stayed in those towers twenty-four hours a day and they had guns. They would shoot anyone who tried to get out. I could not imagine that as I thought guns were for hunting only and I shuddered at the thought of someone shooting at me. Of course my head in the book did not make any difference as we drove past. He may even have slowed down a bit as he retold his terrible prediction.

We arrived at Phil and May's home about the time we would have been eating afternoon lunch in the field at home. May was home as she knew we were coming. I was kind of disappointed when she said we would have dinner when Uncle Phil got home from work. No restaurant tonight! Still, I really enjoyed their home. It was on the edge of town and they had a huge yard with many fruit trees and flowers. Phil worked for Northrup King Seed Company and he was into gardening and trees. I found out years later that when the family sold the home they gave a small amount of land from the yard to the city for a small park. I have yet to see it but it is an adventure I will have as I know it would be fun to go there.

The next morning I could hardly contain myself. The Minnesota State Fair was a HUGE thing. We would spend two days there and it was always early in the morning to late at night. It was a given that we would spend too much time on Machinery Hill, but I could take that because there were so many other things that I liked. I loved the horse barn where I could look and dream about having a horse. Of course we never spent enough time there. I was fascinated with a Ford tractor demonstration. The tractors were just like ours and they did a square dance with hitching and unhitching the plow to the draw bar. They would drive like crazy going forward and backward. I was amazed that they could hitch and unhitch so fast.

We always had lunch at a church diner. Dad would also allow us to have at least one hot dog or pronto pup as we walked around the grounds. This year we took in the fair on Saturday and Sunday. The big final event was the stock car race on Sunday. We watched the entire time and when the race was over we could not believe the winner as we thought a different car had won. In fact we were sure one had lapped the field. The next day, in the paper, there was a big headline that there had been a mistake. One of the cars had lapped the field and the judges had initially missed it. We thought we were pretty smart. Dad was the one who caught it on race day and that made him even more invincible in my eyes. Another thing that was amazing is a game that we watched. It had a large ball on a string. You needed to swing the ball and then on the way back it would knock down the pins. Some people would win but mostly people missed. Dad told Dave and me to come over to the side of the game tent and look. From there you could see that most of the time the man would place a finger behind the pins as he set them.

When he did that nobody could knock the pins down. When he did not put his finger between the pins and backboard the person would knock them down and get the prize. Soon the man told us to move!

The fair was a great time but it was equally fun to stay with uncles and aunts. They led a totally different life. They had nice homes with nice bathrooms. Their yards were mowed and there were arranged flowers around the house. On our farm Mom had flowers but there really was not much arrangement to them. I think the hollyhocks she loved so much grew best near the outhouse or barn! It seemed like they had special food. For breakfast we were served pancakes with several syrups. At home, we had cream or Karo syrup on our pancakes. Even in their work, they did not have to start until well into the morning and could always stop at 5:00 PM! Uncle Olaf was the best. He was always happy, joking around and teasing.

The big city was a wonderland for me. We would get to Fargo maybe three or four times a year, but Minneapolis and St. Paul were so much bigger with tall buildings such as the Foshay Tower in Minneapolis. We went up to the top of the tower one time and people and cars looked like tiny toys down below. We also visited the airport with huge planes all over the place. The planes, the buildings, the people, the sights, all seemed to be from a different world than our tiny farm.

Chapter Twenty-One

MY GOLF COURSE

In the spring of 1959, I was a skinny, shirtless, shoeless twelve year old boy. My older brother Ronald handed me a beat up black plastic golf bag with a wooden driver, a three wood, a nine iron, a seven iron, a few real balls, some plastic practice balls but no putter. When he handed me the bag and clubs he beamed and said, *"Here, Carmen, now you can become a golfer!"* I was excited with anything my oldest brother gave me as he seemed to be God's gift to me. I wasn't sure why he gave the clubs to me, as the nearest course was 50 miles away. However, for the next several years I found ways to entertain myself with them. Actually they took me to places I could only dream of helped transformed me into people who were my heroes.

I examined the clubs that day and then set the bag in the corner of our rickety, rundown shed. I was careful to set them in a place where rain would not get them wet or birds would not do their thing on them. Most of the buildings on our farm were in need of much repair and the old shed, where the Ford tractor was parked, certainly was no exception.

Most of my time was spent on the tractor, but frequently I could talk my dad out of working. On those days, I spent my time with a fishing pole at the nearby lake, making wooden guns or playing Lone Ranger with the ones I had made. I also would often practice my pocket knife skills, play ball or listen to the radio if the St. Louis Cardinals were playing. Now, I had a new "fun" thing to do, play golf. During these years I found ways to have fun alone and with almost no resources.

The clubs sat in the corner of the shed for some time gathering dirt and dust until one day, with nothing to do, I decided I could have fun using them. My creative mind took over and the next several weeks all of my spare time was spent making myself a one-hole golf course in our yard. The distance from our house to the road was 90 yards, which was a decent 9 iron for me. I put a stake in the center of the ditch and with a rope traced out a circle as large as possible, about 12 feet in diameter. Next I dug the circle down about 3 inches. After I had all the dirt removed, I attached the bucket to the back of the Ford tractor and made several trips to the lake for sand. When the circle was filled with sand, I took five gallons of used oil and mixed it into the sand. I knew that would prevent weeds from growing. For the cup, I took an old Folgers coffee can and dug it down in the center of the sand. At that time mom and dad were drinking real coffee and not the instant foamy kind of coffee they drank later in life. Mom lent me an old mop handle to which I nailed a red triangular piece of worn underwear to the top and there was my golf flag. After making a square tee off place near the front door of our house, I was ready to golf. My own private golf course, with no green fees and refreshments in the kitchen just a short ways away!

Wait a minute. I needed something to smooth the sand down so I could putt. I found an old iron cylinder; it had to be heavy, and I attached a wood handle to it. That allowed me to smooth out a wide path from the ball to the hole before each putt.

But I found I had a problem. The width of my fairway was only fifty feet. To the left was Mom's garden and an occasional hook left me among the tomatoes, beans or worse; the flowers. Carefully, I would pick up the ball and take a free lie outside the garden without any penalty. I did not figure I should be penalized just because Mom had decided to plant things along my fairway. However, what I usually did was slice the ball to my right, well beyond the fairway. There the balls would land in uncut grass that tended to get taller and taller as the summer went on. My ball supply consisted of only a few and I could easily lose them all on a Sunday afternoon.

After spending much of one Sunday hunting for balls instead of golfing, I came up with a great idea, kind of a genius thought! After I had lost the last ball, I would go to the dilapidated granary, get an empty 55 gallon barrel, and roll it back and forth. With each bump I would stoop down and pick up a ball. I am sure I had the most inexpensive and efficient ball machine anywhere.

I quickly realized that just hitting balls got old so I invented games. The game I would play the most was Arnold Palmer vs. Jack Nicklaus vs. Gary Player. I would hit three balls and then play them against each other. Arnold Palmer won most of the time. I found I could use the cylinder, that was used to smooth the sand, to Arne's advantage. All I had to do was make the path kind of crooked so that the edge of the path was close to the hole. I was by myself, so in addition to being a golfer I could also play the part of a golf analyst and radio announcer. In my mind I became famous and rich.

After high school I left home and started college where my brother Dave attended. He and I would play golf several times a year. I was always best with my short game, about 90 yards and closer! To this day I am terrible with my driver. After all, who practices with their driver on a 90 yard hole like I made as a boy?

Sometimes I find myself reflecting back on those lazy summer Sunday afternoons. Mom would garden or knit, dad took his afternoon nap and I would become Arnold Palmer. I won championship after championship on my private North Dakota golf course. However, I never really got to cash any big checks!

Carmen, Helen, Dave and Joan
playing in the hayrack before the hay
was pitched into the hay barn

Chapter Twenty-Two

OUR HAY BARN

Let me start by saying we really did not have a "hay barn". That is what we called it, but it was just a large room in our barn. If a person drove down the quiet country roads that went in all directions from our farm, one would see big barns that were built with a second story just for hay. They would have large double doors on the front that would open out. From that a long timber would protrude outward. On that timber would be a rope and pulley which was used to get hay from the wagon up to the second story of the barn. The farmer would then have to climb the stairs each day and throw down hay to feed the cows. That was what a person would see on almost every farm, but our barn was one story, like a rectangular box, with the north partition used for hay.

Our red barn had two big doors on the top of the north end that opened out. It was these doors we used to pitch hay into the barn. We would use the little Ford tractor to pull the hay wagon alongside the barn and then open the doors from the inside. We then used pitch forks to toss the hay out of the wagon into the barn. We often would need to drive the tractor and hay wagon out to the field by Rollof's to fill the wagon. This was done in the winter and even though I loved to drive the tractor I would opt to ride in the hay on the way home because I could snuggle down in the hay, and keep warm. There were times we threw bales into the barn too. I especially liked the straw bales because they were light and I knew that the cows loved to lie in the nice clean warm straw.

Our hay room was actually about forty percent of our barn. When I was growing up it seemed large and inviting. It was a place of much fun, much adventure and a lot of work.

For several years I remember pitching hay from the wagon up through the large doors on the north side. The hay would then tumble into the large room where it would be rearrange it. My job was often to stay in the barn and move the hay around and then trample it down to accomplish the deed of really filling the barn. Of course, the hay just did not magically appear in the wagon under the doors. Often in the winter we would start the Ford tractor, hitch it to the hay wagon which had high sides and then drive out to the field south of the farm. Most of the time this was done in the cold weather when it often was difficult to get out because of the snow. Cold or snow, it did not matter, off we would go with mittens, caps, heavy winter coats and boots. I always had to wear a hat when I left the house but it stayed on only as long as Mom could see. As soon as we were out of Mom's sight, the hat came off except when it was real cold, then those earlaps were put up but the cap did stayed on. Confining clothes always drove me crazy, so often I had to devise ways to skirt around Mom's orders. Each trip we would drive up to the haystack in the field, pitch the hay over the tall sides of the wagon and when the hay was well above the side racks we would head home. I think my brother always put more hay in the rack than I. He did insist on using the largest fork but really I suspect he worked harder than I did. After all, there were always angels to make in the snow, tracks to make around the hay stack with our big overshoes and if it was warm enough maybe a snowball or two. I remember, I could stand a long way from a fence post and throw a baseball size snowball with amazing accuracy. Well, that was my opinion.

Once we arrived back on the farm, we needed to drive as close to the barn as possible so that the hay wagon was right up against the barn wall. That made our work easier, but in order to do that we needed to open the gate and drive half way into the barn yard. We had better be sure to not open the gate too wide as that could, and sometimes did, lead to cows wandering out into the yard where they seemed to enjoy making tracks in the snow. When I was older we would put straw bales in the barn and that was so much easier. I remember well the day dad decided he could afford to have the hay stack moved by the neighbor who owned that huge hay stack moving machine. With that, they backed up to the whole stack, wedged it onto the platform and hauled the entire stack home. Then all we had to do was pitch the hay over the fence and it never entered the hay barn. The trouble with that was it was a constant battle to keep the cows from stretching through the fence. I found out it was easier to keep the cows away from the hay stacks than it was to haul load after load of hay in the winter.

I have said before that Dad was not a farmer but he did have many good ideas. The first year we moved hay stacks, Dad realized at the last minute that one of our stacks was way too large to fit on the mover. Dad's idea was to station the "M" tractor on one side, the Ford on the other and make a rope of barb wire. We flung the barb wire rope over the stack and attached the ends to the tractors. By driving the tractors forward and backward we were able to saw the hay stack in half. That gave us two hay stacks which could be moved to our farm. I think farmers often are brilliant with their ideas.

The hay stack mover changed my life, because now it opened the hay barn for fun. There were sparrow shooting times, basketball time, swing times, jumping off the rafters time and just plain fooling around times. Even when we put bales in the hay barn there was always enough space for fun.

I may be less than accurate when I talk about basketball in the hay barn. It really was a game which consisted of a rubber ball, the size of a tennis ball and a five gallon bucket that had no top nor bottom. The bucket most likely came from some oil purchase so it would have to be cleaned and cleaned and cleaned. Then the bottom had to be removed. The easiest way was to drill a hole, with our antique drill press and then use a metal saw blade to cut around the entire bottom. When that was finished, the entire edge had to be filed so that the sharp edges did not chew up the rubber ball. The top was much easier as it just simply came off. With the top and bottom removed, it then was a matter of getting the old wooden ladder, putting it against the south wall of the hay barn and climbing up to nail the bucket onto the wall. I had to be sure the top of the bucket was ten feet from the hay barn floor, which of course meant all the hay had to be swept clean by the wall. After that it was basketball anytime I had free time to do as I wished. I really think that most of my basketball skills, which were evident in high school, were born in those hay barn days. But I also confess that my dribbling skills never advanced too far. Well, what could a person expect from practice with a little rubber ball!

The barn was a great place to be in the cold winter. The hay, the cows, the cats, and the dog all contributed to a fairly warm place to spend time. I remember one time we had over twenty cats, so that is warmth right there. I have not mentioned this, but Dad wasn't the best at keeping up the old barn. If a window broke it may get fixed, but there was no hurry. The same would be true for a piece of old siding. With a crack here or a broken window there, I was never sure what I may find enjoying the warm confines of the barn on a cold winter day. One thing you could count on was sparrows. Some Sparrows migrate south for the winter but our midwest House Sparrows do not. They depend on human feeders and warm places to stay. The ones I remember headed into our barn and would perch on the rafters as if they were having some kind of family reunion or maybe a political convention. It was always fun to take our 22's out into the barn at night, shine the flashlight and shoot away. I never thought of where the bullets went after they engaged a sparrow but when I think back, that may be the cause of broken shingles, holes in siding and other things that I could never figure out why dad did not fix!

There were many other aspects about the hay barn, too, that were fun in those young innocent days of growing up. I often used the hay barn as a place to lock the dog up or let a calf run around. Sometimes we would make tunnels in the bales or stand on the open ledge of the north doors and jump into the loose hay, kind of reminiscent of a skydiver landing in the ocean.

There were times that I wished we had a magnificent two story barn with a second story hay loft, but I knew our barn was unique and that did make it special. It was a place of work and much fun and I doubt that there were many people who could say they shimmed up the light pole to scout and run around on the barn roof. Wait, that is another story for another day.

Chapter Twenty-Three

THE CREEK IS RUNNING

I woke up with anticipation in the air. It was early May and I knew spring was coming. I was not sure if it would begin today but maybe, just maybe.

Every year I looked forward to the end of winter. Of course there was much to enjoy about winter. A person could argue that winter was full of fun times. I thoroughly enjoyed the sled rides down the hill in the north pasture, the mile and a half walks to school where one could jump into the ditches and land waist deep in the snow, but there was something about spring that brought fun, excitement and anticipation to my soul. The mud; I loved to walk in it. It was great fun digging ditches to channel the water and just plain get dirty. The air seemed to be fresher, cleaner and more alive with birds, animals and the scent of something new. It was always a new experience each spring to walk the road to school and not wear those boots, the black five-buckle ones that did double duty in the barn. I was always thrilled to be able to run fast, stop on a dime, well not really a dime as I had very few dimes, and just feel the freedom of less clothes and more room to run.

But, really what I enjoyed the most and got excited about was the creek. In the lazy days of summer, the creek would slow to a trickle and often totally dry up. When it did that, there would be pools of water in some places, but for the most part there was nothing to dig, to explore or to wade through for fun. I remember days of August when there was really nothing in the creek but memories of the lazy, hazy days of June and July. The spring was different, it was the opposite. I could remember the creek being wide, like the Mississippi River. I guess it was never that wide, but I am sure it was fifty yards or more when it was at its peak. At times like that, there could be water almost up to the fence line near the outhouse. In the summer, it was at least thirty feet from the fence down to the rock dam below, but some springs the fence was so close to the water I could put my leg through the barbwire and touch the water with my boot. One of my favorite places to play was around the bridge which was on the dusty road that meandered towards the lake. In mid-summer I could carefully step on the rocks in the ditch and be under the bridge where it was seldom dry. That area always contained some water where I could usually find a crab or a perch or some other water species. Sometimes, when the creek was at its highest in the spring, the bridge had water spilling over it which made it look adventurous and dangerous.

As I woke up this morning, many of those thoughts were running through my mind. I also thought about the times, when as the water would recede I could walk down the bank, step onto the tiny rock dam and maybe fetch a perch, a sucker or once in a while a northern as they tried to maneuver their slippery bodies over, under or through the rocks. Sometimes they just plain got stuck and then it was fun to grab them and throw them across the dam where they quickly disappeared into the creek and perhaps would, with luck, end up in the lake a half mile north. I would always hope, and maybe pray a bit too, that I could free the suckers before Dad came out to see what was happening. If I could not get there before Dad, I knew that those suckers were goners. Dad would pick up each one, put it into a sack and sometime down the road we would have canned fish for dinner. I think Mom had some kind of magic that she put into the jar which made the entire fish, bones and all, kind of squishy and mushy. Canned suckers were never my favorite food! In my opinion that was totally wrong because those squishy, mushy, soft suckers from the Ball quart jar were next to intolerable. They were not as bad as pickled pigs' feet, but close.

As I scrambled out of bed and jumped into my bib overalls and T shirt, I felt anticipation, curiosity and hope. I had a spring in my step that had not been there during the winter months. I landed in the kitchen from the third step of the stairs and noticed that the bedroom door was closed, so I knew I was ahead of Dad. I dashed through the kitchen where the old cast iron cook stove stood and headed out the door which kind of slammed and banged several times with my departure. Around the house, past the hollyhocks that Mom so dearly loved and then I was on the path towards the creek. Before I could see the creek I could hear it and then there, before my eyes, was spring. The creek was not at its highest, I knew that, but it was up, way up. I could tell by the fence post that the water must have risen at least 5 feet overnight. The rock dam was hidden by the swirling water and the fence beyond the creek was almost submerged.

I stood in awe. There was my spring. No more boots, lots of mud to look forward to and many ditches of running water to play in. I now could run really fast as we traveled the mile and a half to school because there would be no boots. I knew the creek would be there for me in the weeks ahead. Fish to catch, whirlpools of water to splash through and mud to dig in would be at my beck and call for weeks. It would be a challenge, a fun challenge, to find ways to cross the creek when getting the cows for milking and maybe even enough water near the barn yard to drown gophers in the pasture. It usually took five or six pails of water before those darn gophers would come up for air. At that time, I could use a stick to send them to gopher heaven! For me, spring had come and all the adventures I looked forward to were here at last.

Chapter Twenty-Four

MILKING TIME

Many things that happened on the farm are kind of markers in my memories. These markers are often triggered by events or sights or smells in daily living. When that happens, it is fun to go back to those days and relive events for a short time. Sometimes that happens and it takes only a instant to go back but sometimes it is necessary to sit back, shut my eyes and take some time to enjoy what was so important in the past.

I often think of haying when I come across the smell of grass. We had two kinds of grass that we put up into hay stacks. One was a virgin prairie that Uncle Jim owned. The hay was slippery and had prairie needles in it. When you were on the stack, putting the hay in place, you had to push the hay in front of you out to make the edge. If you tried to make the edge by tramping on it you would be in for a slide all the way down to the ground. If the hay stack was even a few feet high at that point you could not climb up as you would just slide down again, so you had to wave to Dad on the tractor and get him to come over with the hay stacker machine and give you a lift on the long tines up to the stack. With the prairie hay, our stacks usually started out a bit wide and then narrowed towards the top as it was necessary to keep a distance from the edges lest you would slide to the ground. The other hay we stacked was alfalfa. This was a hay that you planted as a crop. During a summer we would get two and maybe three crops of hay, depending on the rain. We would make huge hay stacks, the largest in the entire area. Our Jayhawk stacker could go so high that our hay stacks would dwarf other stacks in fields near our farm.

Another trigger that gets pulled sometimes in my life is driving over an old bridge. We had two bridges near our farm. One bridge was on the creek just northeast of our house and we played by that bridge the most. The other bridge was a half mile south of our farm and as the water came from the south and went under that bridge it came onto our farm. It seemed there were so many things to be done around those bridges. The creek was deeper under the bridges so late in the summer, when the creek did not run any longer, there would be water standing under the bridge. It was fun to wade around in the water looking for little creatures. It was also fun just to sit at the edge of the water and throw stones into the water and watch the ripples go out to the edge. Often, at the time the water became very low, there would be small fish in the pools and I would try to locate them and see if I could throw a stone right on top of them. Maybe the most fun was in the spring when the water would get right up to the top of the bridge. We would stand on the bridge and throw sticks or anything we could find into the water on one side and then try to catch them as they came across on the other side of the bridge. The bridge near our house had a larger pond just on the east of it which would often have fish in it. The fish could be easily seen when the water went down a bit in late summer.

One of the biggest triggers for my memory is cows. For some reason I loved our cows. We milked these short horn cows. They really did not give a lot of milk but it was fun having them. Well, at least now it seems as if it was fun!! In the summer, we would have to walk down in the pasture to get the cows for milking. Most of the time we would have to walk most of a half mile, as that is how long our pasture was. About in the middle of the pasture there was a bend in the creek with several rocks on the south edge of the bend. There was this one rock that was mostly in the ground but the top of it was exposed to the south sun. There was a hole by the rock and that is where snakes lived. Our made up name for it was "Snake Rock". We would sneak up on the rock to see if any or how many snakes were lying on the rock to sun themselves. I really had no idea that snakes liked to sun themselves. One time as I quietly walked up to the rock, I saw a snake near the water and just as I approached, it swallowed a frog. I quickly stepped on its tail before it could get back to the rock. I held it up and tied it into a knot and out came the frog and hopped away. When I told Mom she thought I was making it up!

The best, almost romantic, memories of our cows were in the winters before we had electricity in the barn. We would put the seven milk cows in the stanchions, feed them hay from the hay barn and then go into the house to get the milk buckets. By that time, in the winter, it would be dark, so we would take a kerosene lantern from the entryway in the house and light it. With the lantern in one hand and the milk bucket in the other we would walk through the snow to the barn. When I entered the barn, there was warmth coming from the cattle and the aroma of hay and cows was a welcome scent. I would hang the lantern, on a nail in the wall, behind the cows and then take the kickers down. Our kickers consisted of two cuffs connected with a chain. I attached one cuff on a hind leg, brought the chain around the legs and attached the second cuff to the other leg. This would prevent the cow from moving her legs which would have knocked the milk pail over. There was a one-legged milk stool that I would place near the cow and then sit down to milk. It seemed almost instantly legions of cats would appear with their "glow in the dark eyes", looking for milk. It was usually several squirts of milk into the bucket and then one or two squirts into the mouths of the cats. This would continue until I was finished milking. I would then take an old dish and fill it with milk for the cats to enjoy. Carrying the lantern in one hand and the milk pail in the other, I would slowly walk back to the house enjoying the cold refreshing air. We had a milk separator in the entry of our house. I would pour the milk into a large stainless steel container on the top of the machine and turn it on. The cream, almost spoon thick cream, would come out one spout and the milk would come out of another spout. Into the refrigerator it would go to be used on cereal, mush or with bread the next day.

The cold refreshing air, the mellow light of the kerosene lantern swinging in the night, the warmth from the cows and hay, the cats magically appearing out of the darkness and the thick delicious cream gushing out of the milk separator spout made winter time milking an experience to cherish.

Carmen, Helen, Janet, Joan, Ronald and Dave

Chapter Twenty-Five

PLEASE COME HOME

I think that when I was little I prayed a lot. I still do, but when your age is still in single digits I think you may pray in a special way. It could be that when a person is young you do not have the experiences to give you doubts.

We were a family of eight. Mom and Dad were born in 1911, they were married in 1935, Lawrence (Ronald or Red) was born in 1936, Janet was born in 1938, Joan was born in 1942, Dave in 1944, I was born in 1947 and Helen brought up the rear in 1950. In one sense we were one big family but in another sense we were two families. Ronald and Janet graduated from rural Wood Lake School and went to Lidgerwood High School. There was no bus service then, so they would go into town on Sunday night and stay there for the week. I was three years old when Ronald went off to high school and five, two years later when Janet went. The year Joan graduated from Wood Lake there were big changes on the horizon. Our school was down to twelve students in eight grades and the next nearest school, a few miles east, was down to twenty. It was time to close the doors of Wood Lake and bus the students to town. Our farm was right on the border for school districts and we went west to Cayuga, while others went east to Lidgerwood. At that time Janet was finishing up high school and starting college in Ellendale where Ronald was already a junior. Later, when Joan was a senior, Cayuga High School closed and the high school students were bused to Forman which became Sargent Central High School.

I have many memories of Ronald and Janet but not before they left for high school. So the two oldest boarded in high school and the four youngest rode the bus for almost two hours each morning to go to school. I remember a bit about Ronald and Janet coming home for the weekend when they were in high school and that was fun, but of course it was not the same as being home all the time. Mom was such a loving and wonderful mom but she had some very interesting ideas. I would say it was due to the fact that she had not experienced a lot of worldly happenings. Janet was a very pretty gal and I am sure she was popular in high school. I remember Mom talking about all the boys who would come out to the farm on Saturday or Sunday to see Janet. Mom said most of them were Catholic and they were trying to get more people into the Catholic Church. Me, I am positive that was not their motive! Dad had stories of Ronald playing football and how tough he was. I am not sure if Dad drove to watch Ronald play or if he just assumed his son would be tough. I question if Dad watched Ronald because I played about one-hundred and thirty games of football and basketball in high school and Dad never came to watch me. Well, I guess he did watch one of my games. After my last high school football game, which was in Ellendale, one of my teammates told me my dad was at the game. I never saw him and he never said anything.

Ronald and Janet provided many of the firsts in our family because they were the oldest. I am not sure if all the firsts they gave Dad were so important or if Dad just saw something special in them. Ronald, more so than anyone else, could make Dad laugh the hardest, become the most talkative and become the happiest guy in the world.

Ellendale was about seventy miles west of our farm. We would travel to Ellendale several times a year to visit Ronald and Janet. Mom would pack a picnic lunch and off we would go. It seemed like most often we would have a picnic with Ronald and some of his friends. I think those guys looked forward to the homemade bread, Mom's baked cookies, homemade pies and of course the ever present chocolate cakes. One time we had a picnic lunch in a park in Ellendale. Mom had baked a pie which was not a common occurrence. Everyone had eaten and had enjoyed dessert, but there was one piece of pie left. Mom asked if anyone wanted it but everyone declined. Of course, I wanted it but did not say anything. Dave and I went off to play catch but that piece of pie kept coming to mind so I hurried back and announced I would like that last piece of pie. Mom looked at me and said Richard, Ronald's friend, just ate the last piece. For some reason I was totally embarrassed.

One rainy Sunday afternoon, Dad decided we should drive to Ellendale to see Ronald and Janet. It was drizzling, but Mom packed a picnic lunch anyway which, she said, we could enjoy under the canopy in the park. As we were driving Dad asked me if I wanted to see some magic he could do. I always sat behind him so I leaned over his shoulder and was all excited to see Dad's magic. As a nine year old boy I was sure my Dad could do anything. I had seen him shoot ducks, kill deer, change oil on the car, overhaul the engine in Big Red (our old truck), and develop pictures, so I was sure he could do anything on earth. As I sat behind him and waited he said now look at the windshield wipers. It was rainy and the wipers were clearing the window just as they should. He said now if I want them to stop I just say stop and they will do what I say. Well, this was hard to believe but he said "stop" and they stopped. Then he said "go" and they started again. I could not believe it. After he did that several times and had laughed a lot, he explained that the wipers worked on vacuum. When he took his foot off the accelerator it lessened the vacuum and they would stop. When he put his foot down they would start again. I was amazed Dad knew that.

Something Dad did in our family was a huge problem. He seldom would yell and he never used foul language except to say *"What in the*

Sam Hill" but of course we never did meet Sam. What Dad would do is stop talking. It was his way of letting the family know he was angry, as if we couldn't tell! The problem was, often when this happened, we did not know what he was upset about and nobody dared ask him. We could go a day, a few days or even a week and Dad would say hardly a word. He would tell us the work we should do but that was it. It was during these times that I wanted in the worst way for Ronald or Janet or both to come home. If Ronald came home Dad would be all happy and then when he left Dad would forget to be angry again. If Janet and her husband, John, came home it would be the same thing. I remember talking to Dave and Helen and then we might go to Mom. We would ask her if anyone was coming home for the weekend. I remember lying in bed asking, even begging, God to bring Ronald or Janet home for the weekend. It was always special when they came home but at times more than to see them I wanted Dad to talk again.

So, *"Please come home this weekend"* became our battle cry when Dad was upset. As time passed, this changed when tragedy struck in an unexpected way. In the fall of sixty-four Ronald died at the young age of twenty-eight. A severe headache came on when he was teaching, so he went home early. Forty-eight hours later he died of a brain aneurism. Sixteen months later Janet died suddenly at the age of twenty-seven from encephalitis. That took a heavy toll on Mom and Dad and it changed so much in our family. Of course, death is difficult and it takes much strength to deal with it in a family, but over time a person learns to put it in perspective. However, I sometimes sit back and echo the words in my mind, *"Please, Ronald or Janet, could you come home this weekend?"* I also look back at Dad's "silent times" and I try my best to let family and friends know if I am upset and what it is about. When difficult times occur in families, silence is not the way to make things better.

Chapter Twenty-Six

CALLS OF GRIEF

I have never liked to talk on the phone. In my home, it would not be unusual for the phone to ring several times before someone picked it up. I have asked myself many times why I disliked answering the phone. One time I said maybe it was because I did not grow up with a phone in the house. I don't think that entered into the equation. In the nineties I lived a life on the edge and often did not know where to turn next. Maybe that caused me to avoid the phone. I don't think that entered in either. For over thirty years I led Servant Camp and maybe it was for fear of finding out something that I had forgotten to do. No, that was not the case. Then I hit on it. God just did not give me the grace to talk on the phone. That sounds like it could be it but really it sounds more like a cop out. Finally, I have accepted the fact that I simply do not like the phone. It makes no difference if it is a landline or a cell phone, I just do not enjoy talking on the phone. No excuses, no reasons, I just am not a good phone guy.

There are good phone calls, bad phone calls and whatever calls. There was the phone call to let me know I had a new job, that was a great call. There was a phone call from a family member to talk to me about failing in something he truly wanted, a difficult call. There was a phone call from a son who said he had gone to the library to get a book on parenting, a super call. A phone call came from a sister-in-law who cried through a call as she told us a daughter had just died in a car accident, a devastating call. A call came in to tell me I was going to be Grandpa again, a wonderful call. There were phone calls back and forth from the hospital with a loved one, difficult to say the least. In all of these, and of course many more, one does not pick up the phone and expect good or bad news. It usually is just a call for information, to chat or to catch up on the latest. But there are times when that phone rings, you pick it up, and life changes forever without the slightest warning.

Our family was at a Christian gathering on a Sunday afternoon. Some of the kids had stayed home to work on homework, at least they said that was the reason. I was in a school gym worshiping and praying. It was usually a peaceful, grace filled good time with Jesus. I glanced around and there was an usher hurrying down the aisle as the meeting began. He had a phone in his hand and he said there was an urgent call for me. I took the phone in hand and heard my son on the other end saying that Grandpa Lee had called and Grandma had died. Now, Mom had not been in the best of health for some time but it just did not seem that death was near. I had actually felt that we should have driven the 240 miles to Veblen a couple of weeks earlier but the trip was so long and we were so busy. I called Dad back and he seemed pretty together. He said Mom had sat down in her favorite easy chair after a morning snack and did not wake up. That call changed my life for the next several years. It really was not changed so much because of Mom's death but rather the many things that happened in the years following her death. We were sad and we missed her greatly but really the changes in my life coming about because of her death, I could never have imagined. One phone call and instantly life takes a different direction and it is changed forever.

At an earlier time and another phone call, life changed in a big way. It was an unusually warm spring day in April. Sundays were usually reserved for family. We would often go on a picnic or bike ride. The phone rang about midafternoon and the voice on the other end said they were pretty sure our family farm had burned. I tried to call Mom and Dad but could get no answer. A short time later I got another call, this time from Mom, and she said their entire farm burned. Buildings, including the house, were gone along with the equipment. How could that be; I asked. She said they did not know how the fire started but it came from the creek bottom which was dried grass. She said they were not able to save anything in the house. I thought of my Mom's piano, the one thing she loved. It was gone. I thought of the many guns Dad cherished and how they were gone. I thought about his photography equipment, perhaps his most treasured possessions. I knew what little money they spent had been consumed on those things. I pictured Mom and Dad, standing in the yard with equipment burned to scrap metal and house possessions turned to ashes.

I called my school principal, gave him the situation and headed to North Dakota with a heavy heart. Mom had said they were staying at her sister Bertie's so I arrived there about 9:00 in the evening. Dad had just come from rummaging in the charred remains of the farm. He was dirty, covered with soot and looked every bit the man who had just lost all. Mom was fairly composed but so sad. Throughout her entire life she had very little, but now there was nothing. The few mementoes they treasured from Ronald and Janet were ashes. Thousands of pictures were up in smoke and her beloved piano was a twisted heap in a hole in the ground, which had been the basement. I spent the next two days on the farm. It was an eerie place. All was black and where the house had been was just a heap of ashes and dirt. I sifted through the remains, looking for anything that may be salvaged. I came up with Mom's burnt wedding ring, which I think Joan later had made into something. There were some old coins that could be saved but really all was lost. I found out that Dad was able to get into the entry way of the house seconds before it collapsed and he did retrieve two guns. At the age of sixty, Mom and Dad had the clothes they wore to church, their car and that was it. I later found out that their insurance covered some of the house but nothing else. Life changes quickly. In the end, they did not rebuild on the land, they decided to buy a house in Veblen, South Dakota which was twelve miles south of the farm. During the next twenty-five years the move proved to be good for Mom. Was it worth the fire? Of course not, but God can make good out of difficulties.

The third phone call came from my wife. She had a doctor's appointment in the morning. We were somewhat concerned as it seemed to be serious. I walked to the phone in my classroom and listened as she shared the doctor's news. She had advanced breast cancer and action needed to be taken soon. That small call set in motion six years of highs, of lows, of doctor visits, of pain, of diet changes and finally of death. One cannot foresee so many major changes in so short a period of time. Life changes, but for most, life goes on. Phone calls, I just do not like them.

Chapter Twenty-Seven

BIG BOXES AND OLD CLOTHES

I have never been one to put a lot of stock in clothes. I suspect that is really one of my downfalls. I have always liked nice clothes, but most of my life circumstances did not enhance my wardrobe nor make it very attractive.

I remember a few articles of clothing which I really liked and I felt they made me look the good. When I was in college, I almost had a uniform for dress up events. It consisted from top to bottom, a blue mock turtle neck short sleeve pullover, the blue blazer from my high school Letterman's' Club, charcoal gray pants with front pleats and cuffs and brown Bostonian slip on shoes. I wore that outfit to most events that called for a kind of dressy get up and it made me feel great. I remember looking at myself in the mirror before I would go out and saying, *"wow that guy looks great"*. Did I ever hear someone tell me that, not so sure, I am sure I did!

Another item of clothing much earlier in my childhood was a white pullover shirt with three red pin stripes running across the chest. It was not a tuck in shirt and I liked that. I adopted that shirt as my baseball uniform when I played Little League baseball in Cayuga. Somehow it made me feel good, like I could pitch a no hitter any time and hit a home run each time I batted. Well how one feels and how one performs are two different things! I did hit a game winning home run one time when I wore the shirt and maybe that enhanced my perspective. It caused me to consider that shirt as my "lucky" shirt for a few years.

One other item I could have worn every day was a button down short sleeve shirt. I wore that shirt way too often and way too many times. When it finally disappeared, maybe by accident or maybe someone took care to see that it had a decidedly unmemorable ending.

I remember falling in love with a tan long sleeve shirt that had some figures on the front. It came into my possession because it was in included in a tux rental by mistake and rather than make a trip back to the store, I just kept the shirt. I wore it until the elbows had holes in them and people in my family encouraged me to give it up.

What I remember most about my wardrobe were the years I went to grade school and high school. I really do not remember getting new clothes during those years. I would not say I never got new clothes, but it seemed to me that most, if not all, came in this big box that Aunt Ragna sent in the mail. She repeated that gesture regularly, several times a year. In the boxes were secondhand clothes and when those boxes did not come regularly, I am sure I was still mostly in hand-me-downs. I remember disliking my socks because they were always too big and the toe had to be folded over. It seemed to me that the only choices I had in socks were those that were either too big so you folded the toe under or socks that had holes in the toes and those had to be folded under as well! I don't remember being called Lumpy, but I sure felt like a Lumpy with my socks on. As for underwear, well I won't talk about that. Wearing bib overalls was always an option, but I refused to wear them because I never saw Dad wear bib overalls and I wanted to be like him, wearing jeans with a belt. After all, I was sure real men had to wear a belt. For shirts, I am sure there were plenty of old worn ones around that were suitable for church. During the week I did not need to worry because it was always a shirtless summer. If I had a shirt on in the summer, it meant that I was going to church, I was going to town or it was cold outside.

The box; it became something I looked forward to. I do not know how often it came and I do not know if it came to our place first or to Uncle Halvor and Aunt Alta's first. It didn't make any difference to me as all of the younger cousins at their place were girls so the boy's clothes were safe. My Aunt Ragna sent the boxes. I have no idea where she got the clothes or what gave her the idea to send them, but send them she did and it was always a big deal when the "box" arrived. I remember digging and digging into it until we were at the bottom, looking for that almost new shirt that could be worn or those socks that were not too big or were free of holes.

One of the boxes that came when I was a sophomore in high school had a wonderful shirt. I remember, as it was a tuck-in shirt, which was not my favorite kind, but I was at the age where I had no love handles and almost no stomach so I could tuck it in. Being tucked in, it could still feel loose, and I loved that shirt. It had pockets on both sides in the front and I could keep pencils and pens in both when I went to school. Those pencils and pens in the pockets were a habit that I kept most of my professional career. When I taught, I always had an ample supply of pens and pencils in my shirt pockets. I now wonder how many shirts went the way of the rag bag because they had torn pockets or ink stains from pens.

But, back to this shirt that I probably used as my high school uniform for weeks and weeks. I was in Mr. Wohler's study hall in the fall of my sophomore year. I hated to be in study hall and usually I could talk my way out of having that worthless class by getting some extra gym time during that time. However, this day I was stuck in study hall. I really should have liked that class because that would have been a great time to get homework done. After all, there was no place at home to do school work but then maybe I did not do mine too often! Anyway, I needed to sharpen my pencil. I was in the back of the room and the best way to get to the pencil sharpener was to go behind the last desk and walk up the next aisle. I did that, but as I came back to duck between the desk and the open awning window, the back of my shirt, which was most likely way too loose, caught the corner of the window frame. When I moved in front of the window, there was this loud "rip" and I stood there with the back of my shirt completely torn from side to side. Now if I had not been so shy this may have been a time to laugh, but being who I was, the embarrassment was numbing. I know my face looked like I had had just been under a tanning light too long and as I stood there, almost frozen, I felt like I wanted to curl up and disappear from sight. Mr. Wohler, the study hall teacher, came to the rescue. He reached in his pocket, took out a ring of keys that would give a person a lopsided gait, and said I should go to his gym office and get a jersey to wear. He said I could take any one I wanted. I came back, sat down at my desk and for the next minutes until the bell rang, thought about how terrible the experience had been. But, the thought that my favorite shirt gone forever, was devastating.

Chapter Twenty-Eight

SANTA CLAUS DAY

Each year it was the same, each year it was exciting and each year it was a highlight. As soon as Thanksgiving was over, perhaps before the leftover turkey was consumed, my siblings and I would look at the calendar to see when it was coming, Santa Claus Day in Lidgerwood. It was a star event in the year. We usually would combine Santa Claus Day with Christmas shopping all in one glorious afternoon. Dad would give us money so we could buy gifts, and each of us would wander off alone in search of tiny treasures that would become the delight of someone in the family. Wandering off, it only meant walking up and down the many aisles of Dalman's store.

When I was in grade school, I relied on Dad to give me money but when I became a teenager I could spend my own money which I would save from summer work. I would help my cousin Russell or neighbor Rollof with hay bales. They liked to have me help because I was tireless, strong and cheap. I also saved them work and time. Rollof would drive the tractor as I caught the bales coming off the chute. I would stack them five bales high and the width of the wagon so we could make a large load, which saved much time. When the wagon was stacked high, we would drive to the barn where Rollof put the bales on the auger which carried them up to the second floor hay loft. I would be stationed in the stifling hot hay loft to stack the bales as they came off the auger. The times I could not help him, Rollof had to let the bales fall from the chute onto the ground and later he would have to pick them up and haul them home.

When I helped cousin Russell, after lunch he and Uncle Obert would lie flat on their backs on the plush living room carpet for a short nap. I wasn't sure if they really needed a nap or if they just liked the soft carpet, as most people had linoleum in their living rooms. I did not nap but it wasn't a waste of my time because I would talk to Aunt Bertie and by the time those two woke up, I would have enjoyed several of Bertie's homemade cookies. I liked her oatmeal with chocolate chips the best. However, the real reason I wanted to work was so I could save money for Santa Claus Day shopping.

Santa Claus Day in Lidgerwood was a time to see a movie and buy presents. I was not a big spender, as my budget was small or maybe I should say tiny. It was so small I could hardly find the coins in my pockets at times. Before I earned my own money, it would have been usual for Dad to give my brother and me a dollar each. We stretched that dollar to buy presents for Dad, Mom and five siblings. One year I bought a small can of WD-40 oil for Dad and a thimble for Mom.

We were fortunate to have the perfect store in Lidgerwood. We called it the dime store and I believe there were many things for a dime. It was perfect because things did not cost much and it was a variety store so I could find something for everyone. I remember Mr. Dalman, who owned the store, sometimes would ask who I was buying for and he would give me suggestions based on my budget. He actually was very helpful. One time he suggested the can of oil for Dad. He said Dad probably could use it on the farm and he was right. However, with a dollar, it was a challenge to find so many things for so little.

I enjoyed buying presents but the exciting event was Santa Claus Day which was in the movie theater. We did not have a television at home and we never went to movies so that made Santa Claus Day a big event. The show would begin with several cartoons like the *Road Runner, Elmer Fudd* or *Porky Pig*. The main movie would begin after the cartoons. There was always one thing that concerned me. The theater would be packed and I worried that by the time I got to the exit there would be no more bags of candy. That never happened but I was always worried that it might. That probably was the reason Dave wanted to sit near the back all the time.

Businesses in Lidgerwood provided the bags of candy and the people who filled them were kind of tricky. The medium sized brown bags could hold a lot of candy but there was always a big red apple in the middle of the bag. I felt it would have been better to put more Tootsie Rolls or Snickers in the bags but that never happened. After we exited the movie we would take a quick survey of our candy and then put the bags in the trunk of the car. For the next hour or more it was Christmas shopping time.

One Saturday morning, the day of Santa Claus Day, we almost did not get to Lidgerwood. The day started with Dad not in a very good mood. He got that way sometimes. He may have had a headache or it could have been a lack of money to give us for presents. Whatever the reason, he was not happy. We knew it was Santa Claus Day so we were up early and ready to go. Our minds were focused on what to buy for each other and all thoughts revolved around presents. I made the rounds of my siblings asking them what they might like and letting them know that a pack of baseball cards would suit me fine. At a nickel a pack, I even imagined they might be able to afford two!

After Mom's breakfast of pancakes, smothered with choke cherry syrup, we were ready to go. Some of those years there may have been more love than money, so breakfast may have consisted of boiled wheat berries. Shortly after we finished eating, Dad emerged from his dark room, where he had been working on pictures, and asked if we were ready. As we were ready to leave the house he asked if the calves had been fed and the water tank filled. We froze in our tracks and Dad's body language told us we would not be going yet! We already had our good clothes on so we hurried upstairs to change. We raced to the barn. Dave won the race, knowing that chores would not take a long time. We were dismayed that the water tank was so low. Feeding the calves was a five minute chore but filling the water tank took time. We turned the faucet on for the tank, quickly fed hay to the calves and headed to the house to change clothes. We would turn the faucet off just before we left.

With our nice clothes on, our thoughts quickly turned to presents again. After a while Dad was again ready to leave. As he opened his car door Dad asked how much water the tank needed. I looked at Dave, he looked at me and we both sprinted towards the open barn door. We charged into the barn, rounded the corner and stopped short of the tank. There, in front of us, was a second Niagara Falls. Water cascaded over the tank lip into the calf pen making it a swimming pool. After Dave turned the faucet off we walked back to the house. Dave mentioned to Dad that the tank had run over a little but we would clean it up when we got home. Without a word Dad told us to get that pen clean, and fast. A half hour later we were in our good clothes again and racing towards Lidgerwood. We slipped into the back of the theater just as they closed the doors.

When Christmas comes around each year, I take some time to sit and remember. It usually is with my French press coffee topped off with extra Baileys. Nickels, dimes, candy, oil cans, thimbles, baseball cards and much more flood my mind as I journey back to Santa Claus Day.

Chapter Twenty-Nine

GRANDMA SPILLS THE BEANS

When I turned the red and gray Ford tractor into the driveway I was excited. Most of the time my older brother Dave and I were required to work in the fields until sundown, but not tonight. It was the first Friday of the month and that meant Farmers Union meeting night. I really did not understand what Farmers Union was all about, but for me it was fun, games and treats. I looked forward to it each month.

Of course the meeting was nothing, but the treats and ballgame were fun. It always started with, "is there any old business?" and then, "is there any new business"? There rarely was either so then it was on to the program. That always consisted of a sing-along. I enjoyed singing and actually would often sing most of the day as I sat on the tractor in the field. Some people even told me I had a wonderful deep bass voice. We all knew that Rolloff, who farmed a half mile south of our farm, would raise his hand at the beginning of our sing-along and want to sing, *"Sing Your Way Home"*. Everyone would laugh about singing your way home first, but, the piano would start and the singing would take place for the next 15 to 20 minutes. After that there was Kool-Aid and cookies and then if there was still daylight, a softball game with fathers and sons.

Those thoughts ran though my head as I drove the tractor up to the gas pump and turned the ignition off. I could tell it was going to be a pleasant evening as I walked towards the house. The earth and the tall grass were already feeling a bit damp on my bare feet. We still had some tall grass near the house. Just a few days before Dad had brought home our very first lawn mower. Up until then we had used the mower on the back of the Ford tractor, and because of that, many places Mom wanted mowed never got cut.

Once in the house, I was surprised that Mom and Dad were already dressed to go and it was still an hour before the meeting. It took only 5 minutes to drive there as meetings were always in the rural one room school which I attended. Mom said they were not going to Farmers

Union as dad had been asked to show his slides of Washington D. C. to the camera club in Lidgerwood. For a moment I was angry. It seemed I had watched those pictures a hundred times and besides why would Dad choose to show them at camera club and not come to Farmers Union? I knew he loved those trips and to show his pictures to the club was important to him but it also meant that if we had time to play ball after the meeting he would not be there to play with us. But as soon as those thoughts came, I pushed them aside because I knew any ball game was fun, with or without my dad. As they went out the door, Dad said we should be sure to go to Farmers Union and we should walk. I thought, we only had one car, how else would we get to the meeting?

The school was a mile and a half away and we had walked there hundreds of times, so no big deal. I was upset with Dave as he seemed to take forever to get ready. I thought, if he takes any longer we may have to run. After all, I could down my supper quickly because all we were having was hard boiled eggs and bread. I never really tired of eggs as they always seemed to hit the spot with mustard, salt and pepper. My usual supper was 5 or 6 eggs with Mom's homemade bread. Not cream and bread with eggs, just plain bread with lots of Mom's churned butter and maybe a bit of choke cherry jam on top. I think that kind of diet is what made me such a good ball player! Anyway, Dave took forever to get ready but finally we were set. We had ten minutes to get there and we did not want to be late. The earlier the meeting started, the more time we may have for a ball game after the treats. Dave looked at me and said "why don't we drive the big red truck? Dad will never know." Something told me that was not a good idea as Dad had said we should walk but what the heck. We were late and I did not want to short change our ball game. As we got into the big red truck we made a mental note of just where it was parked in the yard. There was tall grass around all the wheels because it had not been used for some time and we never moved it when we mowed the grass. It started right up and we were off to Farmers Union.

We arrived just in time and the meeting went true to form. No old business, no new business and, as expected, Rollof asked that we sing our way home first. It seemed that the sing-along lasted a long time. I was always eager for the treats and then we would have the game. I loved to play ball. I missed Dad in the game because he always seemed to do and say the right things. I thought that when he was young he must have been a really good ball player. He still could hit the ball a long way and usually made the difficult catches and this was when he was kind of old! He even showed me how to throw a curve ball which I never really mastered

The sun set and darkness halted the game with my team winning on my home run over the road and into the far ditch. As Dave and I got into the truck I asked him if he smelled something funny. He said it did smell kind of burnt but really our big red truck was well past its prime. It seemed that it always sounded funny or smelled funny or drove like it was on its last leg. The smell seemed to get worse as we arrived home but we were able to park it in the same spot as before, with tall grass around all the wheels. Walking to the house Dave mentioned that he hoped the truck was OK because there was that smell and some vapor coming from the engine.

We did not hear Mom and Dad come home. Dad must have enjoyed the meeting with his slides as they arrived later than normal. Usually when they went to camera club we would be awake when they arrived home but tonight we did not even hear them pull into the driveway or come into the house. If we had known how late they would be we could have gone into the dirt basement, gotten a jar of Mom's canned peaches and had it for a nighttime treat. We would do that from time to time and then carefully put a new quart jar on the front of the shelf as if nothing had disappeared.

Farmers are known to get up early and work late when there is work to be done but for us kids we just never were early risers. Mom and Dad really never pushed the issue very often. Sometimes during harvest it was up way too early or work way too late but harvest was still a month away. However, the next morning we were surprised when we heard Dad's thundering voice vibrate up the stairs. *"Dave and Carmen, get down here"*. As we scurried down the stairs in our T-shirts and underwear we knew something was up. It even sounded like we could be in trouble. Could dad have found out we used the truck? No way, as we parked it in the very same spot it had been for the last couple of weeks. With no telephone, we knew no one would have told them we drove to the meeting. We could not figure out what was up. As we hit the last step, we were in the kitchen and one look at Dad's face told us he was angry and we were in trouble. *"Did you guys drive the truck last night?"* With faces that almost asked, *"how did you know?"*, we confirmed his suspicions. In a voice to wake the dead, he reminded us about his order that we should walk. He said he needed to haul a load of grain into Geneseo but the truck engine was frozen. At this point, I visualized several years ago when I had cried because I could not go to town with him. It had taken a short trip behind the house and a couple of swift hard swats of Dad's hand to tell me I was wrong. That was several years ago but could this be a repeat? My fears were not confirmed.

As Dad exited the house, in a manner not to be described, we heard him mumble about there being no water in the radiator. When the screen door slammed shut, I could almost smell the foul vapor coming from the truck the night before. With her back to us, Mom busied herself with breakfast. Even though it was my breakfast nightmare, boiled wheat berries that had been soaked in water for a couple of days, I dared not say a word. The taste was dreadful but I ate it all, as did Dave.

When we finished our breakfast, Mom turned from her cook stove and told us dad wanted us out in the field with the rock wagon. Picking rocks was way down on the list of fun things to do. There were times we would pretend to ski behind the rock wagon or maybe we would see how far we could hurl rocks but there would be no games on our agenda for some time. Usually we could delay or wiggle out of an all-day rock picking and make it into a half day, but we figured we best not complain or delay today.

Dad worked for the next two days in silence overhauling big red truck's powerful flat head-8 engine. We toiled in the wheat field picking rocks and wishing the tiny wheat seedlings would emerge which would put an end to rock picking. We later found out Grandma Lee had driven to our place that morning to report her big red truck sighting at Farmers Union the night before.

Chapter Thirty

OUR COOK STOVE

There were many things on our farm that were memorable. Every time I think about the farm, one of the first images that comes to mind is the gas pump. As you came in the driveway you drove right past it. It was a cast iron cylinder with a glass globe on top that would hold 10 gallons of gas. The long handle would be pumped from side to side and the gas would fill the globe. When you had the amount of gas you needed you took the hose, put the nozzle into the tank on the tractor or car and filler up!

Another thing I see in my mind is the wind charger on top of the house. I am guessing Dad wired the house for electricity when I was about four. Until that time the wind charger was used. It would go around and send current into batteries in the basement. Then at night there may be enough current for a bulb or two and the radio for a period of time. When the batteries went dead, it was time to go to bed. One afternoon, when we were in school, in rural Wood Lake, a storm came. I am not sure what we did at school to protect ourselves from the storm. There was no basement and for sure it would not have been a good idea to hide in the outhouses! When the storm passed and we started walking home, we could see that the wind charger on the house was gone. It was about a mile away and we could always see the top of the house over the trees east of our house. We ran all the way home and sure enough, there the wind charger lay twisted and tangled on the ground. At that time it was not used any more but the storm took away, forever, that landmark. Several years later, when we got a bit modern, the television antenna was placed where the wind charger had been. The storm also blew down our shed, where we parked our car and our truck.

There were many other things I remember. There was the white mail box with Dad's name on top. There was the low area in the driveway which was always a mud hole when it rained. It provided hours of fun. The driveway separated the garden, on the north, from a large grassy area to the south where the corncrib sat. A low area in the driveway always filled with water and I would spend hours, after a rain, draining the water from the garden to the grassy area. I would make channels that became rivers as large pools of water drained to the south. In the middle of summer, I would roll up my pant legs after a rain and with bare feet, I would wade in the mud making ditches and channels. I made it into a game and spent hours having great fun!

There was the old, rickety granary that stood near the gas pump. It should have been fixed or torn down before I was born but there it stood with maybe one bin in the middle where you could put coal or barrels or whatever you wanted to stay dry. Well actually, there was another room that we could put baby chicks which didn't leak either, but most of the granary had roof boards gone or siding with leaky cracks where wind and rain would come in.

The thing I liked the most was our old, cast iron cook stove in the kitchen. As the years went by it was taken out and replaced with a modern propane stove that had no character but I suppose it was better for Mom to use. When the cook stove was removed and replaced, Dad took that opportunity to create an ugly rectangular box in the corner of the kitchen which became his haven. He would develop pictures in there and it seemed he would spend countless hours in there often with the door latched from the inside. Not only was it ugly but it really decimated the kitchen décor. That may be a bit strong as the kitchen was as plain as could be, but really, taking out the cook stove and putting that plywood box in its place was a terrible thing to do.

The old cast iron cook stove was many things to our family. In the winter it was a source of heat for much of the house. Even though we had a kerosene stove in the living room, the warmth from the cook stove in the kitchen was always comforting. We could burn old wood, coal, or corncobs in it. Dad would get coal delivered in the fall and it would be put in the granary. We could carry it into the house as needed in the coal bucket, which had a wide mouth bent towards the outside. We could pick up the bucket and pour some coal into the stove. That would be the easiest, as coal would burn for a long time. There was a long time that we would burn old wood in it. The wood from the shed that blew down in the storm was good fuel for the stove. The most fun was in the fall when we would shell corn. We would have a high stack of corncobs near the corncrib. Mom or Dad would sometimes give us a penny for a bucket of corncobs. Those pennies would be saved and we could spend them at the ice cream social at church. The corncobs would burn very fast so you had to keep adding, but they produced a very hot fire.

The reservoir in the stove was a deep cavity on the left side. It had a heavy cast iron cover that you had to lift off to add more fuel. Fuel consisted of corn cobs, coal or wood. On the right side was a large, flat surface that would get exceptionally hot when there was a fire. That was where, in the cold winter nights, we would make the best treats ever. We could get potatoes from the basement. Grandma Lee stored sacks and sacks of potatoes in her basement and when we needed more potatoes we would go get another gunny sack of them. We would have to wash them first as they were always stored with dirt on them. Then we would slice them kind of thin, put a pat of Mom's homemade butter on the top of the stove and fry each side of the potato in the melted butter. Oh my, it was one of the real treats that we could have in the winter. For sure they were much better than your modern day potato chip. We would often make them after supper and before we went to bed. We would also have them after a ping-pong game. We played ping pong on the round kitchen table and when we were finished we would gather around the stove to have fried potatoes.

I was too young to remember, but Dave tells of the time he tried to put the fire in the cook stove out by pouring liquid from a jug underneath the sink. The problem; it was white gas used in the lanterns. Luckily Dad and Ronald came to the rescue and the house did not burn down.

I think the cook stove was the very best way to make pancakes. To this day I can smell the pancakes being made on the cast iron stovetop. When they came hot off the stove onto our plate we could put thick, rich cream over them and smother them with choke cherry syrup. Several were never enough because it took many to fill the voids in our stomachs.

Now there was a terrible side to the cook stove too. That was where Mom would heat the water for dishes! We had no sink, so dishes were washed in a large enamel pan which was used to heat water on the cook stove. As I think about it, I guess that was not the fault of the stove as those dishes had to be done some way.

The old cast iron cook stove went the way of so many other things on the farm. It was tossed aside in favor of progress. It went the way of the forge which I think just rotted into nothing, the wheel that I used to sit at and sharpen my knives and of course the old galvanized tub that was used for Saturday night baths. Sometimes I wonder, what really is progress?

Chapter Thirty-One

DARK DAYS INDEED

Life is full of surprises, changes, heartaches, triumphs, disappointments and victories. Sometimes we are responsible for things in our lives and other times we have no ability to direct or change. I could tell you about situations in my life that were there because I made the wrong decisions and likewise situations that came to me where I had no control over what happened. Some were very sad, some were extremely happy and others just happened as life went on.

It was Friday night and as the bus bounced along highway 12 towards home, I entertained many thoughts. Here I was on one of my last bus rides home from a high school football game. We had just played a game under the lights in Edgeley. It was a game I felt we could win but we not only lost, we were trounced. It was almost as if our entire team was AWOL! I felt somewhat responsible as I was the captain of the team. I had tried everything I could think of but the truth was, our team was barely better than road kill in rural North Dakota. We stunk!

The previous fall we had won the conference. We had lost several key players, yet we still had a nucleus of talent which should have propelled us to a decent season. But here we were with one win and only one game left. Several players had gotten injured but really, I blamed our new coach. The first three years of high school football, Mr. Hanson had coached and he did a great job. This year, Mr. Murray came, not the Mr. Murray from Cayuga, and in my opinion, he did not have a clue as to what a football team should be like. Instead of putting John, a senior, at quarterback he insisted on putting Paul, a freshman, in that position. I knew that would be a disaster and it was.

Even though the ride was long, about ninety miles, it seemed like eternity. In addition to my football miseries, I was concerned about school too. As a senior, I was taking classes that were OK, except for physics. I did not have a clue in that class and there was a big test coming Monday. I did not have great study habits so the weekend was going to be difficult.

We arrived at the school in Forman and most of the players and cheerleaders got off the bus. I had another twenty minute ride, with a stop in Rutland, before we arrived in Cayuga. As I sleepily stepped off the bus, I was hoping Dad would be there so I could go home instead of staying at Grandma's house. I needed to get into my bed and maybe sleep in Saturday morning. That would also avoid Grandma's oatmeal in the morning, which I did not need this weekend. Dad was not waiting for me so I ambled the block to Grandma's house and to my surprise she was still awake and waiting for me. She said Dad and Mom had come by and told her that Ronald had gotten very sick while teaching and was taken by ambulance to Fargo. They thought Ronald's condition was grave so they were on their way to Fargo. Grandma said if I wanted to go home I could take her car.

I took Grandma up on her offer but as I drove, I puzzled and worried about Ronald. It was not like Dad and Mom to drive to Fargo in the middle of the night unless there was a serious reason. Ronald lived in Kulm which was 150 miles from Fargo. Why would they take him that far? Ronald was the person I looked up to more than anyone else. He was eleven years older than I, and it seemed like he did so many things that I really wanted Dad to do for me. I tossed and turned all night and was up at the crack of dawn. We had no telephone, so there was no news.

About noon, Dad and Mom arrived home. As they got out of the car their faces told everything. Dad was stoic and Mom's face was streaked with tears and her eyes were red. Ronald had died on the way to the hospital. That was about all they could tell me. Really that was about all that was spoken that day. I was told that I would not be going to school until after the funeral. No physics test and no football for several days but those days felt like weeks. I remember the time after Ronald's death like it was yesterday. It seemed like hours became days and days became weeks. Our house was like a tomb; dark, quiet and almost eerie. Dad would spend hours in the bedroom with the door closed and Mom would cry more often than speak. I could turn to the right or left, look up or down, but there was no way out. I felt like a prisoner, in for life, and nobody to turn to.

I went back to school on Friday of that week. One of the first things I had to face was the physics teacher, Mr. Henderson. Why did I not bring an excuse and when could I make up the test? I told him my brother died last Friday. In a flustered voice he said he was sorry. He had met my brother the year before as his wrestling team had traveled to Kulm where Ronald taught. I did not know how to act or how to vent my emotions so I said nothing about Ronald's death to anyone. The next week we finished our football season with a loss at Ellendale. I actually played fullback that game and did well but it really didn't matter much. The Monday after the game, one of the guys told me my dad was there. Dad never did mention that he came to the game.

During high school, I played in well over one hundred games and I was not aware of Dad attending any of them. I think he may have had Ronald on his mind that last football game and thought he should see me play once. It could also have been related to Ronald having attended Ellendale College and maybe Dad needed to visit there, I really don't know. The only other time I found out about any interest he had in my sports was after I had finished high school. For some reason I was looking in his kitchen cupboard one day and found the clipping of my last basketball game. I had scored twenty some points and must have played well according to the article in the Lidgerwood Monitor. Dad had cut out the article and kept it.

So ended my high school days and I was off to college. The gloominess of Ronald's death faded but it hung in and around our house all year. At times, I would see a tear in Mom's eye, especially during the holidays. Ronald's favorite cookie was Mom's date filled ones and I don't think she made them for a long time, if ever again. That did not bother me as I did not like them!

I enrolled at NDSU in Fargo the following fall. I really had no interest in college but in those days if you graduated from high school and were not enrolled in college, chances were very good you would be drafted into the military service, so off to college I went. Dave and Marlys were there, Joan and Ron were there as was my sister Janet. Janet's husband, John, was in the army and they had just come back from his tour of duty in Italy. John was about to be sent to Viet Nam as a helicopter pilot. They rented a house in south Fargo and Janet and the kids, Bob and Esther, would live there while John went off to war.

I was overwhelmed with the start of college. There were so many new things in my life and I didn't know how to deal with them. I had total freedom. I did not feel a lack of freedom on the farm, but here I could go any place, and do anything I wanted. It was almost like going into a candy store and having a thousand dollars to spend! I enrolled in the meal plan and there before me was ALL the food I wanted! By Christmas, I had gained fifteen pounds. I was doing seemingly well in my classes but, for some strange reason; I had tested out of math and chemistry 101 in the entrance exams. That placed in advanced classes which were out of my league. The good part was I received ten free credits, the bad part was I understood very little of what the teacher was presenting. I survived, but barely! I had no money so I started working in the Work Study Program as a janitor in one of the dorms. I worked for several hours each Saturday and Sunday. Much of Sunday mornings would be spent checking the halls and bathrooms for messes on the floor from parties on Saturday night! I also would find time to read the Sunday paper, as there was hardly a soul stirring before noon. With all the newness and classes, I did not have a lot of time to see Joan, Dave or Janet although I did baby sit some for Janet. My only transportation was my bike. When winter came, I let out much of the air in the tires so it was easier to ride on the ice and snow.

One Saturday morning, in February, Joan called and asked if I could help Janet because she came down with the flu. I said I could, so I jumped on my bike and rode the two miles to south Fargo. When I arrived, Bob and Esther were up and watching TV. Esther said their dog was cowering underneath Janet's bed and would not come out. I went into the bedroom to see how she was. Janet was barely able to speak but she thanked me for coming. She said she would be better in the afternoon. After a couple of hours, I checked Janet again and she seemed to be worse so I called Joan and Ron. It was evident that Janet was very sick. Ron came over and we decided she needed to go to the hospital. We carried her out to the car and the kids went to Joan's house. I am not sure why we did not call an ambulance, but maybe that was not the thing to do in the sixties.

John was called and given permission to come back from Georgia, where he was in quarantine before being sent to war. Glorine, and her friend Charlie, came the next day too. Of course, Mom and Dad came up. I think Janet died Sunday night or Monday morning. I was in college so I do not know what home life was on the farm but I am sure it was not good for a long time. To lose your oldest son at the age of twenty-eight and then sixteen months later lose your oldest daughter at the age of twenty-seven would be difficult to say the least.

I had no intention of returning to the farm after my freshman year of college. I enjoyed the places I could go and the people I could be with. I also needed to earn money for the next year of college. I went home for Easter and when my Dad was not in the room Mom asked me if I would come home for the summer. She said Dad was really having a difficult time and it would be nice if I could spend the summer with them. I told her that I had to have money and I said I could not come home unless I had some transportation. I knew I would go crazy if I was stuck out on the farm all summer. Mom said she would talk to Dad. The next time I went home Dad took me aside and talked to me. He did not say anything about Ronald or Janet but he said if I came home for the summer he could pay me $500 and would help me buy a motorcycle! Now I thought that sounded like a good deal so of course I said "yes".

That began my motorcycle life of two years. I did work on the farm that summer but spent as much time as I could riding with my friend Larry. I do not know how much, if any, my presence meant to Dad as he was not one to talk about things. I do know that Larry's Honda Scrambler and my Harley Sprint traveled many roads together that summer, of course we were on the bikes!

A person can pick up the phone and their life can be transformed forever. I am sure that Dad and Mom never really recovered from the deaths of two children. How can one? I am not sure. I do know that times like that make indelible impressions on a person. They tend to bring out the worst and the best, often at the same time. From those days and many other times as well, I adopted the expression, *"The only certain thing in life is life will be uncertain"*. Every human life on earth is important to God but the world stops for nobody and life continues on for those who remain.

135

Chapter Thirty-Two

TOP COAT AND HAT

My wardrobe might have been described as interesting. I started out, after diapers, as a T-shirt, shoeless and bib overall guy. I really disliked bib overalls. My Dad always wore real pants with a real belt and I wanted to be like him. When I was old enough, I told Mom I wanted pants with a belt, I never wore bib overalls again. Before I changed to real pants I did find out, through experience, that it is easy to get thirteen eggs in the pockets of a bib overall. In grade school my attire consisted of hand-me-downs from sunny California, hand-me-downs from Dave and maybe even from Ronald. Some days, as I put on socks that were too long and had holes, I thought maybe they were hand-me-downs from Grandpa Lee! In high school, it was same old, same old and I was aware that my attire was a bit "out of fashion". I don't know if it was my makeup or my family values, but my antiquated wardrobe was not an issue. When I went off to college, I tried to dress nicely. For sure, my Bostonian slip on shoes were a step up from my farm boots. I thought they were the neatest shoes ever. My dress uniform was my navy blazer with charcoal pants and a midnight blue mock turtleneck shirt. I really did not try to fit in but I wanted to look nice.

Going back to my senior year of high school and my wardrobe, it was unique and interesting, that is the year and the dress. I had my letterman's jacket for warmth. That would be the right thing to wear to school. After all, I was the football team captain, the co-captain of the basketball team and needed to dress the part. Something emerged in my character my senior year and I decided to be my own person. I would be Carmen and do as I pleased.

During that time my sister Joan was married and working in Fargo. She and her husband Ron lived in Fargo and they were in the middle of a "several years plan" to decorate and fit their house with all the needed items. One day this salesman came to their house to show Joan pots and pans. Apparently, his product was expensive and he did not convince Joan that she needed to cripple their monthly budget just to buy shiny new pans. Not only did he not convince her, but his presentation and attitude made Joan furious. At some point, in the presentation, Joan decided she didn't need the pots and pans and she didn't need the salesman in her house. It was in the fall of the year and cool enough to require an topcoat. Out the door went the salesman, pot, pans and all. Hold on just a minute. Later that day the phone rang and when Joan answered she recognized the voice of the salesman who had left her in a huff! "Excuse me, but I left my coat at your place. I'll be right over to get it?" Joan looked around, saw the nice topcoat lying on her sofa, and quickly told him there was no topcoat in her house. That was the end of their conversation. The next time Joan and Ron came to visit, Joan brought the topcoat with her and asked me if I wanted a nice coat! Of course I answered that I would really like it. I took the coat from Joan, held it up and thought, "I have never had such a nice coat". I tried it on and wow, I thought it made me look special, maybe like a successful salesman! I thanked Joan and took my new prize upstairs to hang it up.

As basketball season approached I had a decision to make. We were required to wear our letterman blazers. The year before our lettermen's club had decided to purchase beautiful dark blue blazers for all the lettermen. The club bought them but we had to pay for them. Our basketball coach, Mr. Wohler, said he would be requiring the basketball team to wear them to all our games. The day of our first basketball game, I went upstairs to get dressed. I put my blazer on, slipped my letterman's jacket over the blazer and thought it looked crazy. I then put my new, fancy topcoat on and man oh man, I looked like a man of the world. I scrounged around and found a hat that Dad had worn some time ago. While wearing the coat, I fitted the hat to my head and it made me look like the million dollar man. So began my senior year of basketball. With topcoat and hat to match, I thought playing basketball would be a breeze! It did not make any difference that the other eleven varsity players wore letterman jackets and the twelve on the "B" team did likewise. My hat became kind of a team symbol. Everyone would make sure it did not get lost and teammates would protect it from getting crushed or flattened out. When I look back, I sometimes wonder why I didn't get teased about it, but when you are the captain and number one in scoring, I guess you are off limits! Then I laugh a bit and think maybe I looked pretty good!

As I think back about my senior year I sometimes ask why. I always have felt that I was kind of a "follow guy" but here I was, perhaps the Lone Ranger in the entire school. My answer always comes back to who I am. I like to be my own person, influenced by others, but live as an individual and stand by my decisions.

My wardrobe, it has evolved over the years to be nondescriptive, but for sure it was influenced by my grade school and high school days. The topcoat, the hat, the lettermen's jacket, the California clothes, the hand-me-downs, and then as an adult, the loose fitting clothes trying to hide the extra weight, my wardrobe evolved over time. All came about in a legacy of change, progress, and improvement, maybe! But wait. I look at pictures of me on my Harley Davidson Sprint motorcycle when I was in college. One picture of me in my blue and white spandex swimsuit, one with my flashy blazer with dress pants and I say, "My dress was pretty neat"!

Chapter Thirty-Three

SPRING CHICKENS

The sound of spring chickens would make my mouth water and my stomach start to prepare for something special. I wonder if that was because spring chickens were so good or if it was just such a step up from mush, hard boiled eggs, pancakes or the other items that were staples in our diet. I think it was because they were so good

Most of the time during my growing up years, our menu did not vary a lot. I know now that Mom did amazing things with the resources she had. I doubt that many mothers could do today what Mom did way back then. There were menu items that seemed so good at the time and then there were things we ate that filled our stomachs but also filled our minds with dreams of better days.

Eggs were always plentiful and we ate them in many different ways. It seemed to me that we would usually have egg sandwiches for dinner (noon meal) on Sunday. Mom would fry eggs with a hard yolk. She would then serve them in sandwiches of homemade bread with a side of dill pickles. I am not sure I would enjoy that now, but then it seemed good. I did not have to make my own meals very often but when I did, it usually was hard boiled eggs with mustard. If I came in from the field for the evening and Mom was not home, which was not often, I would boil six eggs, mash them up with yellow mustard and have a couple pieces of toast with it. Once in a while we would have eggs for breakfast but usually breakfast was pancakes. I really can't mention breakfast without thinking about the awful boiled wheat berries Mom made sometimes. Today that may be a special breakfast one could order in an all-natural espresso bar/foodie place, maybe someone would actually eat that for good health. In the fifties on the Lee farm, boiled wheat berries was the worst possible menu item. I think Mom may have been forced to push that when our entire crops one year were hailed out and we had nothing. That was the year that Dad and Mom had $700 to carry the family over for the year and get the crops in the ground in the spring. Mom made it work but I am not sure how.

Our desserts were always good. I probably should not use the word dessert as we seldom had goodies to finish a meal. Rather we would have bars or cakes or cookies for a snack. It could be a bedtime snack or a morning lunch, as we had a morning lunch and an afternoon lunch when we were in the field working. Actually the best snacks were probably when Mom and Dad were gone and we could eat whatever we found. Cakes were okay but they stayed around for some time. Pies were seldom around but if they were, they probably disappeared. The real snacks were cookies. One was never enough, it had to be three or four. As a final step, we needed a handful as we left the house to head out to the field or to do some important thing like make more wooden guns for cops and robbers. Early on in grade school, when we were still in the rural country school, I remember coming home and Mom would have a plate of double saltines with cake frosting in the middle. I remember talking with Dave and Joan, wondering if Mom would have that on the table as we knew she had made a birthday cake for someone the day before.

It would be easy to assume we would have an abundance of beef but that was not true. We always had a herd of Shorthorn cattle, but we would sell them rather than butcher them. Dad raised shorthorn cattle for the beef and not for the milk. We milked them but they were not good milk cows. I think a shorthorn cow may give one third the milk of a holstein cow. We did not have a lot of beef as they were too important as a cash source. We did butcher sometimes and I remember killing the cow, hanging it upside down on the front end loader and then Grandma Lee making sure she caught the blood for blood sausage! I never did taste blood sausage and I never tasted the head cheese either. It was a big deal when we would butcher. It had to be in cooler weather because Dad would skin the cow and let it hang for some time before we would cut it up. We ate more deer meat than beef. There would be years when we would have three or four deer to skin, cut up and freeze. That was one of my favorite things to do. Dad would do most of the cutting and then I would grind up the meat for burgers. From our deer, Dad would save a few choice cuts for freezing, but most of the meat went into burgers. We had this old hand crank grinder that was kind of hard to use, but I would grind until my arm almost fell off. Of course the best was not the grinding as Mom would always put the fry pan on the stove and I could eat as many burgers as I wanted. That probably was the only time I had an unlimited quota!

When I think of food on the farm, what I think of most often is the spring chickens. It would all start with the mailman, Fritz. Dad would order a hundred chicks and they would be delivered by the Fritz, the mailman. Our mailbox was near the driveway, off the side of the road. Fritz would pull alongside the mailbox, put the mail in, and drive off but in the spring when he drove into the yard, there was excitement. In the back seat of his car would be a large cardboard box with a hundred little, yellow chicks. They were so cute, soft, fluffy and yellow as a canary after a swim in the bird bath. We would take the chicks into the old granary where there was a room that actually had a leak less roof over it! In a pen, we had a large metal teepee looking hood with a light bulb hanging in the top. We would put the chicks in the pen. They would all huddle under the hood where the bulb gave them warmth and peep, peep, peep as if they were happy! It was the kids' daily responsibility to make sure the chicks had water and feed all the time. During the first days we would go out into the granary and hold them, pet them and pretend they were little babies! They grew very fast and it was not long until they were too big to play with.

I do not know how big Mom and Dad would let them get but at some point they would decide the spring chickens were big enough to butcher. That was not fun. We would go into the granary, where we kept them all the time, with a long wire that had the end shaped like a hook. We would use that to hook them by one leg. Then we would take them outside, grab both of their legs, and put the chicken across a board on the ground. It was on the board that we would use a hatchet to cut off their heads. They would always try to strain their necks up to peck us which I hated. After we had chopped off their heads, they would flop around for some time and blood would squirt on us, on the ground and all over the lawn. After they were done flopping around, we would dunk them in a barrel of boiling water. At that point the blood and the smell of hot, wet feathers was almost too much but we couldn't stop, the work had just begun. The next step was picking the feathers off which was a thankless job. Mom would usually "dress them out" and finally they were ready to cut up and freeze. I did not like the process but the end product was delicious. It had to be a special meal for Mom to make spring chicken. Usually it would be a birthday or company or a special occasion because a spring chicken meal was the best.

When I think about choke cherries, wheat berries, mush, eggs, deer burgers and all the rest, what stands out in the memory of my taste buds are spring chickens.

Chapter Thirty-Four

A TIME TO CUT THE STRINGS

The moon lit up the road as we traveled south on U S Highway 81. It was a Tuesday night and it had been a different day, a day that brought many mixed feelings and a day in which I was not sure I had done the right thing. Actually, what brought to mind the entire day, were the lights far in the east. We had left Fargo after an uneventful day, running some errands that Dad needed to get out of the way. I really had not done much of anything. I just kind of tagged along as Dad stopped at Sears, followed by some tractor store and then we had spent maybe twenty minutes or so at Osco Drug where my sister Joan worked. We drove past the Bowler, a café and bowling alley, and then past K-mart on our way home. There would be no supper at the Bowler and no shopping at K-Mart. As I stared at the Fairmont lights in the east, I started to think back on the day.

I had been sick on Monday. I had a cold and felt achy all over. In my mind I had said that for sure it was my bedroom that made me sick. After all, who in the world slept in a bedroom with no finished walls, nails coming out of the ceiling boards above and temperatures near zero in the dead of winter? Of course I knew that was not the cause but it helped to think that way because it made me feel better when I could blame something or someone for missing school on Monday. Who cares about missing a day of school but Mondays were important as it was the day before a basketball game during the winter. I got out of bed on Tuesday morning and as I scrambled downstairs to get out of the cold I heard Dad say something about needing to go to Fargo. The wheels in my head started turning. If I stayed home, but then got better really fast, maybe I would be able to go to Fargo with Dad. While that thought was percolating I also contemplated the basketball game. I knew we were traveling to Fairmont and the chances were very good that it would be an easy game. Basketball came in as the most important thing in my life at the time but then spending time with Dad trumped all. Well, I also had a new thing in my life, a girlfriend.

I paused to think as I stood in the kitchen, wearing my t-shirt and underwear. On this Tuesday, was basketball really the most important thing in my life? I thought about this girl, who I met at the first fall school dance. I now considered her my girlfriend and I had sat with her on the bus going to every basketball game so far. I had to decide what was most important, basketball and sitting on the bus with my girlfriend or riding to Fargo with my Dad. Finally, I asked Mom if she knew what time Dad was leaving. She said he would not be leaving for Fargo until about dinner time, that was noon for us, as he needed to get some pictures finished and put in the mail before he left.

That was it! I would stay home because I was sick. I would get better by midmorning and I would then go with Dad. Maybe he could tell some of his stories when we were in the car. Perhaps we could stop at the Bowler for dinner or supper. We had done that once and the food was really good and you could eat all you wanted. I quickly told Mom that I did not feel well enough to go to school and said I would lie on the couch in the living room. Of course, Mom believed me because she knew I would always be honest. She went about making me toast with a soft boiled egg on top and I settled in on the couch with a book. Dad squirreled away in his dark room working with pictures while shutting the rest of the world out. My timing had to be perfect. If I got well too soon Mom might suspect something and if I waited too long Dad might say that I was still sick. It worked perfectly. About 10:30 I got up and asked for more food. After I ate, I declared myself feeling well and I got dressed. About an hour later Dad emerged from the dark room with his pictures and he was ready to go. I asked if I could go with him and he said he thought I was sick. I said the toast and eggs tasted good and then Mom made a sandwich and that was good too so I felt like I was well! Dad really did not seem that excited but he said sure, I could ride along.

The day was not a good day. Dad did his business and that was it. No dinner at the Bowler, no supper and not one exciting thing during the day. Dad was in one of those moods, the one that meant he was kind of in his own little world. Not much conversation and not any excitement. It was a day that would go down as boring and a waste of my time. But, it would also go down as a day my life took a different path.

146

As we traveled south on 81, heading home that evening, I had many thoughts. I had wanted so badly to spend the day with Dad that I had forgone a basketball game and a chance to sit with my girl on the bus. I was on the freshman team and we had not lost a game. A friend, John, and I were the best players and so far the basketball season had given me some of my "top dog" kind of attitude. I had that kind of attitude in grade school but sitting on the bench during football season had eroded that somewhat. The coach would tell me how well I was playing, there was a girl who thought I was kind of nice and there was some talk in school that John and I would be on the varsity team next year. We most likely would start on the football team in the fall as well. When the lights of Fairmont came into view I just stared at them for a period of time. Had I made the right decision? Even though the day had not one special event in it, I had been with Dad and that really was all I had wanted. Yet, would the game and the bus ride have been more fun?

We turned off of 81, south of Fairmont, and headed west towards home. I was happy to have the city lights behind me so that I would not see them. We drove through Hankinson, then Lidgerwood and finally to Geneseo where we would turn onto the gravel road which would take us home. As we drove the around the curve by Lake Tewaukon, I was glad we were almost home. I remember being quiet as we walked into the house. Mom was still up and she asked how the day was. I think I replied that it was good but really in my heart it was a disaster. I knew that my days of clinging to Dad and to family were waning. Soon, maybe too soon, I would embark on a new and necessary cutting away from family and embark on my own. Perhaps that was the beginning of my life motto, *"The only thing in life that is certain is change"*!

Chapter Thirty-Five

SUPER HERO

As I turned over in bed, I listened carefully to see if Dad was up. I knew Mom would be up as she always seemed to have something to do early in the morning. I never figured out why Mom liked to get up so early all the time and I do not remember ever getting up before she did. I was careful not to make the bed squeak when I moved because I didn't want Dad to know I was awake. Sometimes, if I could pretend I was sleeping, Dad would be out and about and then I would hear the car leave. I knew it was safe to get out of bed if I heard the car leave the yard. Most of the time, in the summer only, I would leave my window open so I could hear better. If I heard the car leave, I knew it was OK to venture down and learn, from Mom, if there was any field work to do for the day.

On the days when I could get away with my little act, I knew it would be a "fun" day. I would instantly start to visualize who I would be that day. Would I become rich, or perhaps be a famous baseball player. I often pretended that I was the "best" athlete in the world. Those things would happen on my baseball field south of the barn, in the barn yard, or on my personal basketball court west of the granary.

There was an electrical pole near the barn and mounted on the pole was my basketball hoop and backboard. My brother Ronald had helped put it up. It was ten feet above the dirt court and was the place where my basketball skills were born, practiced and polished! It also was there that some of the great basketball players of my time crafted their skills. Players like Bob Cousy, Elgin Baylor, Bill Russell, Jerry West and Bob Pettit honed their skills right alongside me. It was funny, as most games we played came down to the last minute and I would always make the winning basket in stunning fashion. Later, I actually used those basketball skills on the high school hard court. However, during my four years of high school basketball, I never really mastered, in a good way, the art of ball handling. I think that may have been because on my court there were too many clumps of dirt and grass to really dribble well.

If it was not going to be a basketball day, it would be a baseball day, and that was my favorite sport. My baseball field was the barnyard on the south side of the barn. If we had rain recently, I was out of luck but, if it was dry I would groom my field and play all day. The south side of the barn was about forty feet wide and about twenty feet high in the center. The siding was lap board siding and fairly smooth for a ball to bounce off of it. The red paint was peeling but that was no problem.

First, I would get the Ford tractor out with the bucket on the back. I loved to work with the Ford tractor. The drawbar was hydraulic so you could lift the bucket up and down and it had a lever for dumping the bucket. I would lift the bucket up as high as it would go and then pull the lever so that the edge of the bucket would scrape the ground. I would drive back and forth several times which was necessary to smooth the ground, and also scrape the cow poop off to the side. When I was finished with that, I would take a rake and go back and forth until I had myself an infield fit for a super star, a hero or a rich baseball player. I did have to go down to the gate on the south side of the barnyard fence to close it. It would not work too well if cows came up from the pasture during the seventh inning stretch!

After grooming the barnyard I was now ready to start the game. This was in the late 50's and I was always a member of the Milwaukee Braves. I do not know why but I was a huge fan of the Braves and I hated the Yankees. It was a great day in 1957 when the Braves defeated the Yankees in the World Series. All of my heroes did their thing, players like Hank Aaron, Warren Spahn, Eddie Mathews, Johnny Logan and the big hero of that series Lou Burdette. They may have been the toast of the town in Milwaukee but each day I could spend in my ball field, I was the toast of the town and the big hero. I had this great glove that Ronald had purchased for me with my money. I remember that it took me at least a summer to save the $10 I needed to buy it. Ronald was in college but he came home often. I gave him my money and asked him to buy me a glove with it. I knew I would not get to a big town to buy it myself. I still have that Wilson glove that to me, in 1957, was almost a national treasure. Today that glove lies kind of folded up in the closet. It looks dated, old and not too useable.

How could a North Dakota farm boy be a baseball hero? I had this ball that was the size of the baseball. It was kind of rubbery so it would bounce well. I had a pitching mound about sixty feet from the barn and hour after hour I would pitch, field, catch, run, make backhanded stops, catch pop-ups and then usually hit a home run in the bottom of the ninth inning to win the game. I never tired of the crowd cheering, of the teammates mobbing me and of the speeches I made after the game. Then when all was finished and I could sit and think about how great I was and what a super baseball player I was, I would dream about how I spent the money they gave me. I really don't remember buying fancy cars or homes but rather I remember going places that I had only read about.

It was fun growing up as a famous person. The hours and hours I spent around the electrical pole and in the barn yard actually helped me in many ways. I was able use the skills on the Little League baseball field, the grade school playground, the football field and the basketball court in high school. Did my dreams come true? Well, not really but I became good enough in high school to be the captain of the football team and the co-captain of my basketball team. In my junior year of high school, our basketball team went to the state basketball tournament. We also won our football conference in the fall. I never became the hero, the super star or the rich guy, but who really cares about the less important things in life.

Happy farmers Carmen and Dave

Chapter Thirty-Six

LAKE TEWAUKON

There always are many childhood events that are worth remembering. It is so interesting how memories come to the forefront. Many times I have been walking where there is lawn work being done and the fragrance in the air takes me back to the hay field in North Dakota. Other times, the view out the window of the car propels me back to the harvest field or the farm yard. However, when I take time to look back on my childhood, there are a few memories that emerge as being more prominent or more important. I could go so far as to say some things had a more important role in shaping me into the person I am today.

One of the things that always comes to mind when I think of growing up is Lake Tewaukon. To clear up confusion, some people called it Skunk Lake, but that was not its name. I think people who used that term were either jealous or not very smart! Some say that name came from the late summer green algae that could have an nasty odor. I would say that happened infrequently and only late in the summer. The wind had to come from the west, blowing towards the east end of the lake, for the condition to become right. When that happened, the water became green in color and not good for much of anything. Swimming was not fun, boating was not very good and if, like me, you used it as your bathtub, you needed to wade several feet out from shore before you would get beyond the green slim.

Lake Tewaukon was a frequent summer destination. It could mean an afternoon of fishing, a spin around the lake on water skies, a personal bathtub or just a bike ride there to see what was happening that day. North Dakota does not have many lakes, so to live a half mile from a lake that was about a half mile wide and three miles long was a treat.

I would say the most important use of Lake Tewaukon was using is for our bathtub. We had no indoor bathroom on the farm. One summer we made an outdoor shower. It stood west of the house, kind of in the trees. It had three sides made of old weathered boards. We cut the top off a fifty-five gallon barrel, painted the inside black and put a faucet in the bottom of it. We ran a hose out to the shower and filled the barrel with water in the morning. By evening we had a nice warm shower. We did that the summer my brother Ronald and his wife Glorine lived with us. Ronald came up with the idea. Most summers we did not have any way to bathe easily except the lake. In the winter we would get the galvanized tub out Saturday night and place it in the living room. After it had been half filled with water, we took turns taking a bath. When the last person was clean, well kind of clean, we carried the tub out and emptied it. So really the best tub we had was the lake in the summer. Most evenings, after working in the field all day, we would take a towel, a washcloth, soap and hop on our bikes. Dave would ride the big bike and I would ride the little bike. We would wash in the lake, swim for a while and then ride home. We could hold the bath items in one hand and not touch the handle bars all the way home. We took pride in riding from the lakeshore to our front door without touching the handle bars. I have to say that in August, when the algae was the worst, it may have been a fair question to ask how clean we were. However, if it was harvest and we were in oats or barley, anything was better than going to bed with harvest dust covering our body. I remember, Dad would often come in the house after a long day of harvesting, eat a bite and fall asleep in bed. I could never figure out how he could do that because it seemed the dust from the grain would make me itch, nonstop. The worst was oats, it seemed to invade every pore of my body and make me miserable. When we were harvesting oats or barley there was no choice, we had to get to the lake every night.

One of my favorite things to do at Lake Tewaukon was water ski. Ronald had a boat that could pull a skier. John also had one. It was during my grade school days that I learned how to ski on two skies, then on one ski and then become skilled enough to try and do different things on the skies. I thought I was pretty hot stuff when I could hop on one ski and ride the wake of the boat around Lake Tewaukon. I would ski as far to one side as I could and then pull hard on the rope to cross the wake and see how fast I could go. Was I as good as I thought I was? Probably not!

Fishing was another activity that we often enjoyed at the lake. For some reason we never fished, for real, on the east end. We always had to go to the west end just off of the bridge that sometimes in the spring was under water. I do not know how good Dad was at fishing but I am sure he felt that you had to fish early in the morning. It seemed we always had to wake up way before sunrise and be fishing as soon as one could see the bobber. Most of those times we really did not need to see as we would cast the red and white Dare Devil for northern pike. If it was a good day, we may go home with a couple northerns that were in the five pound range. Then if we were so lucky to bring fish home Dad would skin them, never fillet them, and we would have fish for supper with a great portion of bones! To this day, I am sure northern pike have more bones than any fish in the world.

Another favorite activity at the lake was to go to the east end where there was a bridge. The water was usually deep enough to jump off the bridge and pretend we were so great or so brave. We often would do that towards evening and then as dusk set in, there would be hundreds of fire flies in the weeds. We knew that would be the case, so we always had a jar with us. We would catch several and bring them home to see the jar light up.

Sometimes we would bike up to the lake just to see if anyone was there. One time Dave and I rode our bikes up and there was a young couple kind of far off on the north shore of the lake in a grassy area. We stopped and kind of hid ourselves to see what they were doing. We really did not get a good look at what they were up to but as much as we saw we decided we need not see more! Another time we rode up to go swimming and before we got in the water we noticed a picnic basket near a tree and it appeared nobody was around. We thought how could someone leave a full picnic basket by the lake. As we looked more closely we could see a boat far out on the lake. Naughty as could be, we sneaked over to the basket, took some store bought cookies and rode away as fast as we could.

Lake Tewaukon also had tremendous choke cherry trees. There were times when we went up to the lake with five gallon pails and came home with them full. Mom would boil them, use a colander to get out all the juice and then she would make choke cherry jam and choke cherry syrup. Choke cherry syrup was delicious on cream and bread, pancakes and mush.

Lake Tewaukon was also the site of our annual, end of the year school picnic when we were going to Wood Lake School. There would be a picnic and then a softball game on the hilly area east of the picnic tables. We would have home plate by the road and would bat uphill. A home run was over the hill.

The lake was also our recreation center in the winter. With our shovels, homemade hockey sticks and pucks we would walk up to the lake. After we had shoveled the area clear of snow we would place our overshoes for goals and have a great hockey game. If we were not in the mood for hockey we would bring our fishing gear and ice fish. I am not sure how many we caught but it sure was fun digging holes and putting the line in. It also was cold sitting on those darn five-gallon pails. When we were brave enough we would sneak into one of the unoccupied fish houses and fish. It sure was warmer in there.

Lake Tewaukon, the memories are many and the stories are fun to tell. After I left home, the Federal Government came in and bought up all the land around the lake. Soon there were signs up that said "no fishing", "no swimming" and "no boating". I guess one could say that it truly was "for the birds" after that. Its washtub days were over.

Chapter Thirty-Seven

TEMPTATION AND FAILURE

It was a perfect day. The North Dakota sky was a brilliant blue. Unlike the day before, the air was calm with a hint of the summer hay season peacefully floating from the south alfalfa field over our farmyard. I knew it was going to be a good day. Mom had made eggs for breakfast and as she flipped them over to the sunny side she mentioned that Dad would be gone all day.

That meant I had some big decisions to make. I knew Mom had one idea for me, that was to take the hand cultivator and walk through the garden. Even though it was work, I enjoyed that over picking the weeds from between the plants. I also knew that I could finish that in short order. Then I would be free all day to play. As I walked out to the haystack near the barn I didn't even step on any chicken poop, so for sure it would be a special day. I had made a tiny cave-like hole in the west side of the haystack and that had become my "thinking cave". It was not hidden or anything, it was just a place I could sit and be me. I had made it on the west side of the stack, so as I sat there I could see the calves. I loved those calves and would sometimes put a rope around their necks and parade them about the yard, pretending I was showing them at a world's fair! Life was good. I settled in to my own little space and started to think of all the options I had for the day.

I heard the car start and as I glanced out I saw Dad back up to the gas pump. Soon, very soon, I would have the day to myself. Then the car was shut off and out of the corner of my eye I saw Dad walking towards me. I did not know what he might want, maybe some work he thought of. By the time that thought crossed my mind it was too late to escape. Dad approached and I could tell by his face that this was a good thing. To my surprise he asked if I wanted to go with him. I loved to spend time with Dad but for some reason I had no desire to go to Cayuga or Lidgerwood or Geneseo. However, when he mentioned that he was going to Oakes, I sat up. Oakes was forty miles away and we seldom went there. Dad said he had some things he wanted to see at the implement dealer. I jumped up and said I would be ready in two minutes. I had bib overalls on and I would not be seen in public wearing those. In a flash, I was changed and sitting in the front seat of the car with Dad. Little did I suspect that I was embarking on a day that would impact my life forever.

I seldom had Dad to myself so this was a real treat. But, I also had other treats in mind. Perhaps a burger, an ice cream cone or maybe a real banana split! Dad was in an unusually good mood. Often, when we drove some place, he would seem to be deep in thought, but this day he was talking almost non-stop. We even went the long way so we could drive past Silver Lake to see if the fish were biting.

We stopped in Forman on our way as Dad had a dividend check from Farmer's Union to pick up. I think that is what he was so excited about, because he had some money to spend. We arrived in Oakes about noon and I had high hopes for a burger. Dad did not disappoint me. We stopped at a tiny café on the outskirts of town and went in for lunch. We did not even look at the menu. Dad ordered a burger and fries for both of us. I had a glass of milk and Dad had black coffee. I thought the milk tasted different as we milked cows at home and our milk was much richer and creamier. From the café we headed to our destination, the International Implement dealer.

When we entered, Dad said I could look around as he needed to talk to a salesman. I strolled up and down the aisles with little interest until I arrived at aisle #5. There, stretching from aisle #5 to aisle # 7 were more farm toys than I had ever seen in my life. There were tiny Ford tractors, just like the real one at home. There were big and little trucks, some even had a box that would move up so you could dump the sand out when you were hauling it in the sandbox. There was a tiny road grader that would be perfect with my toys at home. I thought I must have arrived at the North Pole.

From the farm toys, I wandered into the last aisle and there were more toys and games. I picked many of them up and examined them from front to back and top to bottom. As I picked up one game, something dropped on the floor. It rolled under the shelf so I knelt down to get it and there in my hand was the shiniest, brightest and best marble I had ever seen. I knew if I had that, I could knock down more empty shells than Dave when we played our soldier game. We had nothing that would be comparable to it in our Mason jar of marbles at home. I wanted that marble in the worst way. It had fallen out of the box, I knew that. Did it really belong there? I tried to rationalize why I should keep it. I looked around the store and nobody was in sight. I slowly put the brilliant marble in my pocket and headed out to find Dad.

I found him standing at the counter talking to a man about seed corn. He finished shortly and we headed out the door. As we walked towards the car I held onto my new marble in my pocket. I knew I should not have taken it but I just could not help myself. Halfway to the car, I could not resist the temptation to take it out of my pocket to see it in the sunlight. As soon as the marble came out of my pocket, I heard this deep voice sound an alarm. "Where did you get that?' I sheepishly looked up at Dad and started to cry. I stood there on the sidewalk with my hand out, my head bent and tears streaming down my cheeks. I was able to mumble, "I took it from the store". Dad did not blink an eye. He knelt down beside me and in his most stern voice said we had to go back to the store. He told me I had to bring the marble back, go to the manager and tell him what I did.

It was the last thing I wanted to do but with Dad, there was no talking back, no arguing and besides, I knew I was wrong. When we arrived back at the store I managed to tell the man I was sorry and I would never do it again. When I handed the marble to him it nearly fell on the floor from my sweaty damp hand. As he scolded me, I felt like I shrunk from a tall 6 year old to a little boy again.

We drove home in an eerie silence. I never understood if Dad was angry at me, if he was ashamed of me or if he was questioning where he went wrong in raising me. Perhaps all of those things went through his mind. Oakes was forty miles from home but the ride home seemed like a hundred miles. When we drove into the yard, Dad said we did not have to tell Mom. I do not remember if I ever told her but I do know that I never stole anything again.

Chapter Thirty-Eight

MY MOTHER-MY NURSE-MY DOCTOR

Most everyone has a mother. Well I mean everyone does have a mother. What I want to say is my mother was pretty much everything to me and my siblings. We lived ten miles from town, we lived twenty-five miles from high school, we had one car that was gone much of the time and we had very little money. In my childhood "no money" meant no insurance, very little extra food and a minimum of frills. That may have been true for many families but I think our family had less than most. I believe we were the last family to get a phone, the last family to get indoor bathroom facilities and so it may be correct to call us the "last family". We could have been the "last family" but I always felt loved in a big way.

What does a mother do if there is little money, no insurance and someone in the family gets hurt? Of course, if it would be a life and death situation you hurry to the nearest doctor or hospital, but if it is not life threating you simply fix it the best way you can. I remember two times Mom took Dad to the hospital. One time Dad was oiling a chain on the combine during harvest and "oops", his hand went between the cogs of the wheel and chain. That was not pretty but very serious, so Mom drove to town with Dad passed out in the front seat. Another time Dad was starting the combine engine. Our old pull type combine had this great sounding engine mounted on the right side of the combine frame about eight feet above the ground. The way to start it was to climb up the front of the combine, pull out the choke, turn the run button and push start. After it started and ran for a time, you would push in the choke and you were ready to roll. Well, Dad didn't exactly keep things in the best way and the battery was dead, so he needed to start it with a crank. To crank the engine, you had to climb up the ladder behind the engine, step out and away from the combine frame and put one foot on the large combine wheel while balancing the other foot still on the ladder. You then had to reach up and with a mighty jerk, none of us kids were strong enough for this, pull down on the crank. It may take several times before the engine started. One time the engine backfired and the crank handle came back and sent Dad sailing through the air and onto the ground. He was able to get into the house before he passed out. The combine sat idle in the field while Mom drove Dad to the Lidgerwood hospital.

In those situations, Mom drove Dad to town but if I, or one of my siblings, were injured it was usually Mom, the doctor, on call! This story is about my mom, a.k.a. the nurse and the doctor. I and my five siblings lived through grade school, high school and then left home with not too many scars or permanent physical handicaps so I think Mom did a pretty good job. Well, may sister Joan did have polio and to what degree I do not know. I am sure Mom and Dad did what they thought they should, but was it the best thing? I guess only Joan knows.

Epson Salt seemed to be the fix-all and magic potion of the time. I remember many times coming into the house with a rusty nail or screw fastened to the bottom of my foot. No, it did not go through my shoes because for me summer was barefoot time. I did wear shoes to church on Sunday as Mom insisted that was only right. Each time my foot had something in it that did not belong the routine was the same. First, you had to sit down and Mom had to get it out. The instrument of choice was determined by the object. Most of the time it was just grab and pull it out, I mean it does not take even a super mom to look at a foot, see a nail in the foot and then just pull on the old board that is attached to the nail! Mom's medical instruments consisted of a tweezers and in some situations, a needle. She always had to sterilize the tip with a match before she probed deep into the wound. There were also times that the object could not be gotten out and then it would be up to the Epsom salt to bring it near the surface. First, the tea kettle needed to be filled with water and put on the stove. When I was quite young, the tea kettle sat on the old cast iron cook stove but when I was a bit older, we upgraded to a four-burner propane stove. Sometimes, Mom would see us coming and put the water on before we got to the house. Most of the time, Mom got the object out of my foot or hand by the time the water was hot. We had a large metal bowl which was the doctor's bowl. That was where Mom would put the salt and hot water. When the salt was totally dissolved, in went my foot or hand for several minutes.

The bad part of this was, I usually would have to listen to mom tell me about the importance of wearing shoes. She knew I was not going to change but I guess mothers have to do things like that. The good part was if Mom had time there would be a treat while I sat. No Twinkies, candy bars or M&M's but rather a slice of bread with jelly on it or maybe some saltine crackers with leftover cake frosting. One of Mom's frequent treats for us was to take leftover frosting from a cake or batch of cookies and place a big dollop of it between two saltines. That was kind of like a poor man's Oreo! At the end of the sitting time, it was usually "thanks Mom" and I would be off. These medical emergencies seemed like a minor inconvenience when I was growing up and in fact they were something I did not mind at all because of that goodie. I think if they were to happen today it would be a different story!

There were times when more than Epsom Salt was needed. Perhaps, one of the most dramatic times was on a beautiful autumn day. I remember the leaves had started to fall, there was a welcome aroma of smoke in the air from the burning of sloughs and ditches and the late afternoon sun smiled peacefully in the southern sky. It was approaching deer hunting time and the rifles were out, shined, cleaned and ready to be sighted in. I was too young to go with the men hunting but dad decided it may be a good time for me to shoot the deer rifle for the first time. I had my own 22 rifle but I had never shot a deer rifle. I loved to handle my gun, clean it, take it out and shoot at anything from rocks to boards and even blackbirds. Actually I got quite good, a few years later, at downing blackbirds. Dad handed me the deer rifle. When you shoot a 22 it has no recoil, meaning the stock does not jerk back into your shoulder, so how was I to know that this deer rifle had BIG time recoil? I have asked myself many times, why didn't Dad instruct me, but at the time it was not a thought. Dad instructed me on what to do. You make sure the safety is in the "on" position first. Then you take the rifle with your left hand and place it on the stock under the barrel. Put your right hand around the stock and your pointy finger in the trigger guard. Rest your cheek on the butt end of the stock, ease off the safety and fire!! The deer rifle had a scope, so I had to get real close to the lens to see through it. When I pulled the trigger, I thought the whole world had exploded and come up into my face. What happened was, the scope kicked back to my face and cut a neat half-moon over my right eye. There I stood in shock, with my right eyelid drooping over my eye which was covered with blood. I think that should have been a "doctor time" but no insurance usually meant no doctor visit. Instead it was a bit of a scolding from Dad and then into the house to Doctor Mom, who must have done the right thing. I think she went big time with a cleanup and a real band aid. I survived fine with a covered eye and a headache for several days. Over time, my eye brow concealed the scar so it was not noticeable. To this day I would like to ask Dad why he didn't explain what would happen when I shot the gun and why the scolding?

One of my most memorable "sick" times was when I had the mumps. I must have been in the fifth grade or so. I remember feeling so sick and it seemed like Mom was always there. There would be Vicks on the chest, a cool wash cloth over my forehead and an extra blanket or quilt if it was needed. Meals consisted of a soft boiled egg on toast or maybe homemade tomato soup. Mom's medicine kit included Epsom Salt, Vicks, soft boiled eggs and toast, a band aid if there was a real need and then much love and always a homemade quilt to keep warm. Well, there were always extra cookies or crackers when I was mended enough to enjoy them.

I have to admit that more than once I took advantage of sick times. Perhaps it meant an extra day at home or maybe a special treat. It seemed that Mom was always so busy with many things but when I needed medical attention, that was a time when I felt like she loved me the most. Some alone time with Mom, or just a kind word were, always part of the doctor's medicine and it certainly helped the healing process.

Chapter Thirty-Nine

SECRET TREATS

When I was growing up, a treat was something that did not happen often but when it came my way I enjoyed it immensely. I remember what my dad would do during harvest time. There were times we would haul oats or wheat or barley or rye home and put it in a steel bin, but more often we would haul it directly to the grain elevator in Geneseo. Dad always drove the truck to town when we were selling the grain. There the truck would be unloaded and Dad would get a check for the sale. When Dad drove to town he would leave Dave and me in charge of filling the combine tank. Dave would drive the tractor which pulled the combine and I would sit in the stubble as Dave circled the field. At the perfect time, I would jump up and race across the open space, catch onto the ladder on the back of the combine and climb up to push the grain away from the auger in the 50 bushel tank. Sometimes I just sat high up on the combine or stood in the tank but that was not so much fun. It was better to race across the field to reach it just in time. There were actually two reasons for that. One was, I would try to time myself so I would reach the combine, climb the ladder and get to the tank as the grain touched the auger. The other reason was I loved to run across the field where there were thistles, rocks, large sticks and other things that were always in my path. I always went barefoot in the summer and it was always fun to race across a thistle patch and never feel the stickers on my leather-like feet. I guess I would say different strokes for different folks!

But, the real deal was when Dad returned in the big red truck. He would drive up to the parked combine. We would then open the chute on the bottom of the tank to unload the grain. Our "Big Red Truck" would hold 150 bushels, the equivalent of three combine tanks, and to me that was a lot. I knew the neighbor's truck held twice that but I though our little truck was better! When we were finished, Dad would climb on the tractor and my brother and I would get in the truck to drive to where we thought the tank would be full again. As my brother slid behind the wheel of the truck, I would get to open the dash to see if Dad had left a candy bar for us. Often it would be kind of hidden in the dash, but peeking out so we could easily find it. What we called the dash is today called a glove box. It did not happen every load but often enough to make it exciting. That was always fun but the really big treat was the day we finished harvest. Dad would drive the last load of grain to Geneseo and when he came home there would be a case of root beer soda on the truck seat. Wow, that was the ultimate treat for the summer.

Another treat was when Mom would go with us to Lidgerwood or Geneseo to get groceries or to just go for a Sunday drive. We knew that if Mom came along, there would be a very good chance Dad would stop at Fritz's store on the corner of Highway 11 and Highway 14. There we could have a delicious, huge single-scoop ice cream cone. I remember driving out of the yard and heading north around the lake and then past Marble Grove, an area full of trees. As we would drive around that curve and head north, my mouth would begin to taste that strawberry flavor. I always preferred strawberry over chocolate. The thought of the coolness of the ice cream would make me forget about the terribly hot summer nights when it was too hot to sleep in our bedroom. I would also think about the ice cream that Mom would make. She would mix up milk, eggs and vanilla and then freeze it in metal ice cube trays. When we wanted ice cream we just pulled the lever on top of the tray to loosen the cubes and dump some in a bowl. I liked it but her ice cream did not compare to store ice cream, which was flavored and of course scooped on top of a sugar cone. Yes, I did like Mom to go with us. It is too late to ask Mom now, but I actually wonder if the ice cream she made was really ice cream or some other concoction. Mom did have a way of making treats for us which we thought were great, only to find out in adulthood that the "treats" which we loved were kind of iffy!

There were other treats too. Dad liked black licorice candy. I never did figure out if he really liked it or just liked to watch the kids or grandkids eat it and get their faces all black. Fritz's store in Geneseo always had these black sticks of licorice which were in the shape of a tiny pipe. Dad would buy some when we stopped and they were always delicious. It was also fun to pretend to smoke them!

Another treat was a Baby Ruth candy bar. Now that candy bar was over the top in size. It came in a white and red wrapper and was a whole four ounces. I mean, that is a quarter of a pound of pure delight, if one can make it last for an hour or so. I remember I used to tear the end of the wrapping off and then take a tiny bite. I would wait as long as possible and take another bite. There was one day when I made it last almost the entire day. That was really rare, as self-control has never been my strong point, but it did happen occasionally.

Another treat was play time
Joan, Carmen, Dave

All of these treats seemed to come and go and they were always appreciated, but for sure the most enjoyable treat and the one that seemed to be at the top of my list was the secret one. Well, I thought it was secret, but later in life I found out that it was no secret at all. I should have known but what does a ten-year-old know about secrets any way. My mom would work hard all the time but she was more busy than usual in the fall. Before we got our freezer, she would can chicken and fish but most of her canning was about the garden produce in the fall. When garden produce started to come in, Mom would spend days in the kitchen canning beans, tomatoes, beets and more. On many hot summer days Mom would stand in her "non air-conditioned kitchen" taking quart jars in and out of her pressure cooker. Starting in early August, about harvest time, Dad would bring home crates of peaches. Of all the food Mom canned, I loved the peaches the most.

One of the great things about peaches was they always came with this thin paper wrapping around each one and that paper was perfect for the three-holer. That paper was so soft, it beat the yellow pages hands down. Actually, that is another story.

I remember Mom putting the peaches in hot water, then taking the skin off and slicing them in half. By the end of fall she would have many quart jars full of these delicious halved peaches. They were stored in our basement, which was really a cellar with dirt walls and floor. The cellar was under the living room. To get to it, you needed to open the narrow pantry door, squeeze past the sink where Dad shaved, open the trap door in the floor, prop it up and then descend down the steep, wooden steps. The water pump was on the east side of the cellar and opposite that were shelves where Mom stored all of her canned food. I think, because the floor and walls were only dirt, it was not unusual to greet a lizard when you reached for a jar of food. I never did become friends with those slimy looking green things.

The times that Mom and Dad would go to the neighbor's house or to camera club we longed and waited for because it was when we were alone that we felt we could have our secret treat, those delicious peaches in the cellar. Dave and I would argue a bit to see who would go into the cellar. Who was brave enough to go into that dark, dirty confinement where it was musty and the lizards were waiting to stare you down? Finally, one of us would decide it was worth the risk and down we would go. We would eye the shelves where the peaches were to see if there were enough left so Mom may not notice if a jar went missing. We would then carefully take a quart jar and move the one behind it to the front of the shelf to make it look like all was well. If we were lucky, we would not encounter any lizards. We then scurried up the stairs to enjoy. As we savored the last peach half, and licked the plastic bowl clean, it just seemed that life was good and to think nobody would ever know! Only years late, when I was talking to Mom, did it dawn on me that we did not fool Mom for a minute. She knew all along what we were doing and I suspect she was happy that we enjoyed the fruits of her labor so much.

Chapter Forty

MY ULTIMATE GIFT

I have gotten many gifts in my life time. Some of them have been just what I needed. Some of them have been just want I wanted. Sometimes the need and want are the same but often they are totally different. I know that there have been times when I received a gift and I was very appreciative but other times when I was not. I know a gift is an act of appreciation or an act of love towards another person and one should always be gracious but I know I have often failed.

As I share some of the gifts I have received, I will not share the giver for many of them. I just think it is best that way. I think it is always good to assume a gift is given out of love.

Early in my adult life we would exchange gifts with many people. It seemed like family and friends alike would often take the time to share something. It did not have to be a big gift but rather the act of giving seemed to be the most important thing. One Christmas I received this package from a family member. It was wrapped nicely and after I read the card I was excited to open it. As the wrapping paper came off and I stared down at the gift, I did not know what it was. There lying in the box in my lap was something striped with multiple colors. Slowly I reached down, picked it up and still I could not make out what it was. I then held it up and there before my eyes was a red, green and white striped vest with a rainbow colored belt around the waist. I slowly put it on and it felt like I had transformed myself into a circus clown but had forgotten the big shoes! I never wore it of course and I am not sure I sent a thank you note but I probably did.

One of my most used gifts ever came from my mom. I am sure she talked to Dad and he was in on the present too, but for some reason I always gave Mom the credit. It was her idea and most likely she had to convince Dad it was a good gift to give. It was an electric blanket that kept me toasty warm many nights in my bedroom. I can still see myself racing up the stairs, two steps at a time, getting out of my clothes in record time and jumping into a warm bed as the bedroom air delighted in making the nails in the roof above me look like a crystal chandler. After I had set the record for undressing and getting into bed, only then, would I take the time to glance at the radio clock to see the time. In the winter I always had to check the time because the radio clock tended to slow down when the temperature dipped below freezing. I actually did not have to worry because I knew if I did not get up at the right time, Mom would call upstairs. In the morning, I needed to roll out of bed, get dressed and be ready to stand by the driveway waiting for the bus by 7:10. If I was late, the bus driver, Ray, would be kind enough to drive into the yard, but I really did not like him to do that as I felt it made me look lazy.

Another gift I did not really understand and I am sure was not fully appreciated was when I finished graduate school in 1976. I worked hard to get my master's degree in special education. There were night classes at the junior college in Devils Lake, an entire summer of classes at the University of Nebraska in Lincoln and three summers away from family as I went to school in Grand Forks ND. During those days I stayed with an uncle and aunt one summer, with friends one summer and by myself one summer. I had no money to eat out and for sure I would never stop for a cup of coffee. What I did was bring a cooler full of food on Monday morning when I left home to drive the hundred and ten miles to my first class at eight in the morning. Most of the food came from our garden. I would eat out of the cooler all week, as I was often able to get all my classes in by Thursday afternoon. That meant I could have a three-day weekend with family.

I remember sitting in the park in Grand Forks pretty much every day while I ate my lunch or dinner. By that time my vocabulary had changed so lunch was my noon meal and dinner was my evening meal. On the farm lunch was at 10:00 AM, dinner was at noon, lunch was again at 3:00 PM and supper was in the evening Come to think about it, I never should have gained weight because as I grew older I eliminated one lunch and never had supper!

The gift!! It came about two weeks after I graduated in July. It came in the mail wrapped like maybe it was something special. I was very curious to see what it was. It was not large like what my Mom and Dad had given me. They had given me a gun case for the shot gun I had purchased from Dad. I really liked that and I needed it too. Here in the mail came this little package about the size of a paperback book. I opened it with great anticipation and there was a used paperback dictionary!! I am really happy that only family was there to see my face and maybe hear my words although I probably was speechless.

I still recall some birthdays when I was growing up. It seems like I was a little young to remember when I was two years old but I think I do. It may be only because I have a picture, that I remember that birthday, but I got three cakes. I got one from Mom, one from Aunt Bertie and one from Aunt Alta. I don't know who ate them but I am sure they did not last long. I still have the picture and I look really happy. I also have a picture of what Grandma Lee gave me for my birthday when I was six or seven. I would always have cookies when we visited Grandma so she must have thought she would be really nice to me. She drove over for my birthday and gave me a cookie about as big as a cake. It was the biggest and one of the best cookies I ever had.

The ultimate gift came about a week before I graduated from high school. Grandma Lee was special to me, as she was to so many people. I stayed with her many nights during high school when I would often get back to Cayuga after a football or basketball game late. There would be times when Dad was sitting in the car waiting for me, but if I did not see Dad, as the bus pulled in at midnight, I would walk the block to Grandma's house to sleep for the night. In the morning

Grandma would always fix me oatmeal but I long ago forgave her for that! The oatmeal was edible but she insisted that it had to have raisins which I thought was a terrible idea. Anyway, I spent many nights at her house and she was always fun, happy and loving. As graduation neared, Grandma became sick. I am not sure what her illness was but Dad drove her to the Veblen Hospital and it seemed she may not live too much longer. About two days before graduation, we drove to Veblen to visit her. I was not that comfortable in the hospital room as maybe many young people would be, but just before we were to leave, Grandma asked me to come over to her bedside. She took my head in her hands and gave me a kiss on the cheek. Then without saying a word, she put her hand into mine and pressed a twenty dollar bill into my sweaty palm. I said "thank you" and as we walked to the car I am surprised that the twenty dollar bill did not melt as I squeezed it so hard. The gift; it was not large, but who gave it to me and how it was given made it my ultimate gift!

Chapter Forty-One

WEEDS AND ROCKS

Our farm was in southeast North Dakota. Some of the land we farmed was a scant mile from the South Dakota border. Just on the edges of that land were "the hills". If you drove over the hills, you were in South Dakota. To the east, the Minnesota border was forty miles. If you were to leave our farm and drive thirty miles east and a bit north you were in the Red River Valley. The Red River Valley has some of the richest farm land in the world. Families with land in the Valley were considered wealthy. What about our land? It put us into the "land owner" category but not the wealthy one!

Our farm, well, it was an interesting story. Mom and Dad eked out a living on our farm. There were many reasons for our family not thriving in rural North Dakota. Dad had little interest in upgrading or improving our farm. His heart and mind were all about hunting and photography. I don't know if he curtailed his hunting and photography because of money but I do know there was always a shortage of money to improve the farm. Another reason for our relatively poor existence was the size of our farm. Mom and Dad owned a quarter and a half and we farmed another eighty acres owned by Uncle Jim. Even in those days, the fifties and sixties, three hundred and twenty acres was a very small farm operation. Of that acreage, some of it was creek, pasture land and hay land. I think most mid-size farms had at least four quarters of farm land, which would be six hundred and forty acres. I do think we could have earned much more money from our farm, if we had just done some things differently. I can talk about where Dad's heart was and I can talk about the size of our farm but really the land was not choice land by any stretch of the imagination.

The farm buildings were on the east half of the quarter we owned. The buildings included our house, the barn, a small shed, a large dilapidated granary, a chicken house, a corn crib, four steel bins and I must not forget the three-hole outhouse! We had a large yard with a shelterbelt of trees on the east side of the house. To the north there was a small grove of trees, not any bigger than to hide the outhouse. There was a large fenced barnyard. A creek ran through this east half of the quarter and surrounding the creek was our pasture. Beyond the pasture, to the north, we planted a large shelterbelt of trees and to the east, across the road, there was another long shelterbelt of trees. West of the pasture, was farm land that was a half mile from north to south. On the east side of the farm, beyond the shelterbelt, was our half quarter of farm land.

A short but accurate description of our land would be to say it had many sloughs, which were good for ducks and pheasants, and it grew weeds and rocks as well as wheat, rye, oats or barley. Our grain crops were usually adequate and occasionally they were great. But, the rock harvest was always a bumper crop!

First the rocks; they seemed to be everywhere and of course they do not grow but it seemed like they did. I imagine they were dug up each year in the fall as we plowed the field after harvest, but really there was no end to them. There was a short time frame that we could pick rocks. Some of the progressive farmers had mechanical rock pickers that they pulled behind the tractor, but Dad had human rock pickers who were fed pancakes in the morning, sandwiches at lunch and mush for dinner! The crops were planted as early in the spring as possible. The stubble that was plowed in the fall was left to lie like that during the winter. In the spring we would disc it, smooth it out with a drag and then plant crops.

The time frame after planting and before the crop emerged was "rock picking time". We could not pick rocks after the crops emerged because the tractor wheels would ruin the new tiny, tender plants. I think that time was about ten days or two weeks but it seemed much longer! We had a rock wagon. It was a four wheel wagon with heavy timber for the bottom and side boards that were about ten inches tall. That would allow us to put as much weight in the wagon as the tires would accommodate.

I should say that rock picking was not all bad. We were smart enough to make some games of it. The bottom line was, it just was not fun picking rocks because the next day it seemed like there were as many or more still in the field. Making games of it helped pass the time. We were always barefoot and it was fun to hold onto the back of the wagon and slide on our feet as one of us drove the tractor. It was usual to pretend the rocks were shot puts and see how far we could throw them. At times we would find killdeer bird nests and we would try to catch the bird, which we never did. We may start in the middle of the wagon and see how high we could pile the rocks on it. When we arrived at the creek, where we disposed of the rocks, the game could be trying to hurl and hit a certain rock someplace or just seeing how far we could throw them. Of course we never did this in much of a hurry! I am sure I started picking rocks when I was six and when I left for college, twelve years later, there were still rocks to be picked.

Weeds were another pest. Dad seldom sprayed with chemicals, so often our fields were infested with weeds. I don't know if he didn't believe in chemicals or if he did not want to spend the money. I remember one year he hired a plane to spray the crops west of the house. How do you get rid of the weeds without chemicals? Well, you work the land carefully before the crops come up and then you wait and pray. We often had weeds and Canadian thistles in our crops. They would bloom about harvest time. Thistles had pretty purple flowers, which turned to cotton-like flowers and emitted a smell that was pungent. They would lie in the rows of cut crops and as the combine fed everything into the auger, the air would be filled with flowers that would blow under your shirt, into your nose, and places one does not like to mention. When I was driving the tractor, pulling the combine, I would hope and pray that when I came to the thistles, there would be a head wind so they would blow behind me and not in my face.

One of the things I would do just for fun was to run bare foot through what we called "sticker patches". I would go without shoes all summer so the soles of my feet would be like leather. Running through the thistles or stickers would not faze my feet at all. We had many sloughs on our land and the thistles tended to grow near them where there was water. If it was a wet year, Dad may not be able to cut close to the sloughs and therefore the thistles may not get into the crops. However if it was dry, look out, those cotton-like flowers would blow up, down and everywhere!

Our farm land, it gave us enough to live on. I think we could have done much more with it but then what about the memories of weeds and rocks? The memories of weeds and rocks are great today but in bygone years they were a big reason I did not like farming.

Chapter Forty-Two

GRANDMA & GRANDPA

Every young girl and boy should have a grandma and grandpa. I was blessed to remember three grandparents. My Grandma Sampson died before I was born but Grandpa Sampson, Grandma Lee and Grandpa Lee all gave me lessons and memories that are still with me today.

Grandpa Sampson died when I was in grade school. He lived in Veblen, South Dakota with Uncle Jim. They had this spartan like house that I thought was great. The basement was large, with no clutter, a pole for support in the center and a toilet that actually flushed. The toilet sat in the middle of the basement with no room around it so when I used it, I had to be watchful! As a person came into the house, you went upstairs and entered the kitchen. There were white, metal cupboards and on the edge of the sink hung a leather strop for Grandpa's shaving. There was a plain wooden table with wooden chairs on the two ends. From the kitchen, you walked into the living room with its wooden floor and a scatter rug in the middle of the room. Grandpa always sat in the corner, near the window in his rocking chair with his spittoon nearby on newspapers. It was evident that newspapers were needed in case of a miss. There were two bedrooms, one for Grandpa and one for Uncle Jim. There were very few pieces of furniture or pictures in the house but everything was always neat, in place and clean. Outside, their garage could be driven into from either side. On the north side of the garage was the outhouse which always smelled better than our three-holer on the farm. Mom would drive us to Veblen to visit Grandpa and Uncle Jim about once a week. The first thing Grandpa would do when we arrived is give us a hug, a kind of stiff Norwegian one, and then he would pull his bar of chew out of his bib pocket. He would offer us a bite and then give us his hardy laugh. As we wrinkled our noses at the smell, he would take a healthy bite and put it in his pocket again. While Mom visited, we would play outside around the garage and outhouse. Having no indoor toilet at home, we would always make sure to use the basement toilet, even if there was little need. Often we would do more exploring than playing, but I always liked to be at Grandpa's place. If it was cold or rainy weather, we would play in the basement. It always seemed to me that there was so much space at Grandpa's house and so many things to do.

My favorite story about Grandpa Sampson is one that I was not a part of. The story took place when Grandpa was a young man. He took a load of grain into Geneseo with a team of horses in the winter time. One the way home he met a neighbor and neither would pull their team out of the ruts in the road to allow the other to pass. What do you do? Well you get off the wagon and duke it out to see who gives! He arrived home looking like a disaster and when Grandma asked him what happened, he muttered something about those darn horses took off on a run and he fell off the wagon! I am not sure it is true but it certainly is a fun story to tell. I think farmers in the roaring twenties often settled differences with their fists, but perhaps red headed farmers were most likely to do it! I remember Mom being very sad when Grandpa died. I thought she must have loved him very much.

I spent much more time with Grandma and Grandpa Lee. I think part of the reason was they lived closer and part of it was we just spent more time with the Lees than with the Sampsons. They lived on a farm about three miles from us until I was in fourth grade. Then they sold the farm to Uncle Halvor and they moved to Cayuga where I went to grade school. I remember part of the reason for moving was that Grandpa was beginning to have health problems. Grandpa was a giant of a man, maybe six-feet-four with arms that seemed to reach from wall to wall in their house. His arms seemed to be able to reach anything and his hand could grip three large potatoes, a turnip, a kohlrabi and a bunch of carrots all at the same time, it seemed! I am not sure how Grandpa earned money on the farm but then I suppose he was retired when I knew him. I can still see him on his little International tractor. With his huge frame, his long arms and big hands, he made the scene look like some child was on this toy tractor in the dirt pile.

The most endearing thing about Grandpa was his laugh. He would throw his head back and give a belly laugh that could be heard for miles. The thing about it was, his laugh was so genuine. Grandpa just seemed to have a wonderful outlook on life and he was always happy. He died when I was in the sixth grade and that left me with one grandparent, Grandma Lee. Grandma was the cookie person, the berry person, the hugs person and the concerned person. She was pretty much everything a child needs in a grandma. On the farm she had a garden as large as a small grain field. Every fall we would have potato day. Grandpa would drive through the potato patch with his one-bottom plow and then grandkids would walk up and down the rows filling large gunny sacks with fresh, red potatoes. Grandpa would then carry them into the house and down into the basement. Anytime we needed potatoes we would drive to Grandma's to get a sack.

Beyond the garden, she had her berries. I remember currents, strawberries, raspberries, gooseberries, blueberries and there must have been more, too. It was a great time when we could go help Grandma pick berries and she never scolded us for eating too many. In the back of her house she had plum trees, apple trees and even a pear tree. Grandma always had cookies too. Mom would remind us not to ask for cookies as we drove up into the yard, but really there never was any need to ask because there was a plate of cookies on her table all the time. There would even be one for the road. Well, that may have to be asked for!

When they were still living on the farm, we would often go over there on Saturday nights. Dad, Uncle Halvor, Aunt Alta and Grandpa would play cards while Mom and Grandma visited. The kids would play games in the house or out in the yard. When we got tired, instead of begging to go home, we simply would curl up on Grandma and Grandpa's large bed and fall asleep. Mom and Dad would wake us up when they were ready to go home.

After Grandma and Grandpa moved to Cayuga their life was very different. I suspect it was a difficult move for both of them. I remember Grandpa sitting out in front of the house, enjoying the warm summer weather. He always appeared to be happy, but deep inside I am sure he missed his farm, his little tractor and their large garden. After Grandpa died, Uncle Henry moved in with Grandma and actually for the next six years, I spent more time with Grandma than ever.

For the first couple of years after Grandpa died I would often play Chinese Checkers with Uncle Henry. When I got good enough to win most of the time, Uncle Henry lost interest in playing. In high school, I would often sleep overnight at her house because the bus would drop me off in Cayuga, sometimes as late as midnight. Grandma made the best pies, cakes and cookies, but her oatmeal was terrible. Of course, I would never have been so rude as to tell Grandma I didn't like it. Most mornings I would hold my breath with each bite, that was because she insisted on putting raisins in it. One morning she asked me how the oatmeal was and I said very good so she plopped another scoop in my bowl. From that time on I made sure to answer that it was good, but I was full!

Grandma died a few days before I graduated from high school. I remember helping to clear out her house. Aunt Amanda came from California to Grandma's belongings. I don't know what happened to my beloved Chinese checkers game but I think about it often. As I watched Amanda pile rugs, dishes, furniture and other items into her car and a rented trailer, I wondered if she realized how many memories those items gave me. I remember wanting to ask Dad if I could keep something, the Chinese checkers maybe. I realize now, things can be taken, but memories are forever.

Chapter Forty-Three

CHRISTMAS PROGRAMS

Each year when Thanksgiving was over and we marched into December, my face would get kind of sad and my attitude was terrible. Don't get me wrong, I loved Christmas. We did not get a huge haul of presents each year, but I remember we would get something and it usually was an item we wanted. I remember one year I received a clock radio and I really thought it was the best present ever. When I was in high school, I received an electric blanket which was a most welcome present with the temperatures in my bedroom free falling to near zero in the winter. However, December meant going to Bergen Church every Saturday for hours of practice on the annual Christmas program. It was not a favorite time for me.

I should have been happy because I think it was the happiest time of the year for Mom. She loved the piano and her dream was to play the piano/organ in church. There was this elderly farmer named Eldon, who had been the church organist since the cows came home for milking! Mom thought he should have retired by the time I was born but no such luck. Each Sunday Eldon was there ready to lead the singing with his organ playing. Mom told me his hands were so full of aches and pains that he had to soak them in Epsom Salt water before he came to play. Now that sounds a bit funny and I have no idea if it was true but I know Mom was honest. Occasionally, Eldon was sick or maybe he ran out of salt, whatever the reason was, he could not come to church so Mom did get to play.

So the Christmas program was a big deal for Mom. She was in charge, she chose the music and she got to play the piano for the entire production. She did a great job even though we did the same scenes, wore the same clothes and sang the same songs each year. The only change would be who was cast as Mary this season, who was cast as Joseph or who got to play an angel this Christmas. Come to think of it, I never was cast in the role of an angel!

This is how things worked. Thanksgiving would come and go and then it was Saturday afternoons at Bergen. For the next three or four Saturdays before Christmas, we would drive the few miles to Bergen Church and remain there under Mom's watchful eye for hours.

I remember Bergen Church well. We would leave our driveway, drive the half mile south to the corner and then head east. We would go around the Olson slough, stop at the intersection, which was where we would turn south again if we were going to Veblen, drive past the Tosse farm and then turn right as if we were going to visit the Quams. It was then only two miles to Bergen. Before we arrived, we had to drive through a low spot in the road that would often be covered with water in the spring. I used to hope it would be that way on Sunday because maybe we would not be able to get to church. I should not have felt that way because we really had a good deal going. Our pastor had a church in town and two in the country. He would have a town service every Sunday and then alternate between Bergen Church and Palestine Church so we had services every other Sunday.

I didn't dislike church that much, but I sure was happy when I was old enough to not sit with Dad and Mom. When I got to be high school age, I was allowed to sit in another pew with Chuckie, the only boy in church my age. Our big thing was to each have our own song book and each time we sang a song we would see who could open their book closest to the correct page. I think I won more than half the time! Bergen Church was really a big part of my childhood and for sure, material for more stories in the future.

Back to our Christmas program, that is what this story is about. Mom really did do a good job, but I don't think it was necessary to practice and practice and sing and sing each Saturday afternoon for the entire month of December. First, everyone had to get dressed in the costume they were going to wear. Then this scene had to be rehearsed, followed by another one and then another one. When all the scenes had been gone through we would march up to the front, that is if we weren't already there, and sing. I mean we would sing "Joy to the World" and then "Old Little Town of Bethlehem" and then "Come All Ye Faithful" When we sang that song I would wonder about the unfaithful! It seemed to me that each time we sang the song we did a good job so why we needed to practice and practice, I can only come to the conclusion that Mom loved to play the piano. When Chuckie and I were not up front, most of the afternoon was spent sitting and talking about school. He went to Lidgerwood School and I went to Cayuga School so we would swap stories much of the time. That was kind of fun but I remember wishing I were home playing in the barn or reading a book or playing cards with Dave, something useful or fun.

There was always a gift exchange after the Christmas program, which happened on the last Sunday before Christmas Day. One year I almost crawled into a corner, I was so embarrassed. I felt that should be a time when one could expect some kind of toy or game or something interesting. I was in a small group of boys, standing in the rear of the church, before the program. We probably were talking about how glad we were to finally have the program and not have to practice each Saturday. Somehow, we got on the subject of the gifts and starting talking about what we may get. There was always a name draw so nobody knew who they would be getting a gift from. I mentioned that I sure hoped I didn't get a pair of socks. I was tired of folding over the toe of most of my socks, so a new pair would be welcome but somehow it did not seem like that should be a Christmas gift. In fact, as we stood talking, I could feel the lump of sock under my toes! After the program, we had the gift exchange and there in front of me was a new pair of socks from one of the guys I had been talking to. I really should have gone over to apologize but, of course, I didn't. Instead I avoided him the remainder of the evening and the topic of gifts never came up again.

My Mom was a wonderful woman and mother. I always felt bad for her that she never got to be the church organist. It seemed that she had so few desires in her life and most of the ones she had never came to be. Years after I left home, to be on my own, I realized that my attitude towards those darn Christmas programs was terrible. I don't think I ever told Mom that, but then I suspect back in those days I probably was able to hide my boredom and maybe, just maybe, came across to Mom as being the nice son that I so badly wanted to be.

Chapter Forty-Four

THE CLEAN UP

I have never been accused of being the neatest person. In fact there may be family members who would say I certainly tend to be fairly unorganized and messy. I would not dispute that but, as most people, I am a work in progress and I am getting better. I would go so far as to say that much of my past history is partially a result of my environment and is not the real me.

Perhaps I should blame my lack of orderliness on my upbringing. Why not? That could actually be true. But really the following is unfair so I will not do that. Some mental pictures of my childhood are these:

My dad loaded his own rifle and shotgun shells. Did he have a room or space or a real place to do that? He did not. The ritual was when he loaded shells he sat on the stairs leading to the second floor. We had to step around or over him on the way to our second floor bedroom. When he was finished did he carefully place all of his equipment away? No, what he did was store them in the floor joists where his powder, shells and bullets remained until he, or a friend, needed more ammunition. It was not a neat or orderly way to do things

Dad built a dark room when the cast iron cook stove was taken out. To the day I left home, his dark room was left unfinished and stood in a corner of the kitchen as a reminder of things undone.

Mom and Dad's bedroom was just large enough to get in on either side of the bed. At the end of the bed was a dresser that allowed one to squeeze past into the closet which had boxes and piles of stuff. I often wondered how they could find anything.

It seems like I am painting my parents as some kind of misfits who lived in this home with no order and no rhyme nor reason for what they did. That actually is not the case. They were caring parents who I loved dearly. They lived their adult lives in a small house with little money to upgrade or improve things. Is that an excuse for disorder? Probably not.

I just want to build a case for myself if I ever declare all things that are wrong with me came about because of Mom and Dad. I am not saying that now, but I am holding it out there just in case!

Really, my story today is about a hog barn that I never saw. Our farm yard was ninety yards from the road, almost the length of a football field. As you drove in from the east there was an old dilapidated shed straight ahead. Near that was the gas pump. The gas pump was a glass cylinder with gallons marked on the glass. The glass was perched atop a rusty, round iron pedestal. The storage tank was underground. To fill the car, or tractor, I had to pump a long handle from side to side, which brought gas from underground up to the glass cylinder. If you wanted ten gallons, you just pumped and pumped until the gas reached the ten gallon mark on the cylinder. Then you took the hose down, put the nozzle into the gas tank and pulled the lever. North of the shed and gas pump was the house. Beyond that was a garden spot which Mom filled with flowers. Immediately behind that was our three-holer, that glorious out-house. A bit west of the three-holer was a small shed which usually housed the Ford tractor. You could walk south from that shed and come to the barn in about one hundred and fifty steps. Between the shed and the barn was our hog barn that I never saw. How could there be a hog barn if I never saw it? If it ever did exist, why was it not there when I was growing up? The story was, we did have hogs and really their home was there. It had a large cement floor with footings all around. I would say it was maybe thirty feet wide and sixty feet long. There was some kind of hog disease that went through the rural area and wiped out the entire hog population. I never did hear if a storm blew the hog barn down or if it burned down. All I know is for the first many years I lived on the farm there was this huge, ugly slab of cement that stood in the yard as if it defied all comers who desired to clean it up. Weeds grew up, around and in it but there was very little one could do to make it look nice. I often heard Mom talk about how ugly it was and how nice it would be to clean it up. Because it remained there for so long, I assume Dad had no interest in beautifying our yard.

I am not sure how it came about but I think it was like this. My older brother decided he wanted or perhaps more accurately, needed, to get away for the summer. Really, quite a smart idea, as he found a farmer about one hundred miles away who needed a hired hand. It certainly was more inviting to go work for money than stay home. I was thirteen and what was I to do? Dad would have work for me but I knew there would often be spare time. When school was out I made a decision, the hog barn foundation was going to go that summer. I knew Mom would be pleased. My mother told me she did not think I could do that by myself but I replied that it was not a matter of can, but rather how!

I knew how I would attack this monster cement slab. Our "M" tractor had a front end loader on it. That is what we used to get large rocks out of the fields and also what we used to hang a cow, up high, when we butchered. Regardless, I knew I could use the loader. We had a large hammer maul and I would need our huge log chain as well. I decided the cement needed to join the rocks on the creek bank to the east. We had a rock pile across the road and beyond the shelterbelt. Along the creek bank, was where all of our rocks were deposited, kind of like rock heaven. I am sure that creek bank is the final resting place for thousands and thousands of rocks. That rock pile contained very interesting rocks too. Some were missiles, some were shot puts, and some were flying saucers. As we picked them from the field, they magically were transformed into different objects. This rock heaven would be the final resting place for the hog foundation.

For much of the summer, I longed for days when Dad would not direct me into the fields. Each morning I would hope that I could spend the day hammering, breaking, chaining and hauling. The cement was broken into big, small, round or flat slabs. They were then hauled in the front end loader or dragged with the log chain to the rock pile. I remember how excited I would be with each trip. When I arrived at the rock pile, I usually had to get the chain off the cement and then lower the front end loader. I would then say some goofy slogan and push the cement over the creek edge to see where it would land. I would envision a clean yard, with immaculate grass, each time a slab of cement was deposited in the rock pile.

I started on the northeast corner of the hog barn and worked my way west and then south. When I got a piece of earth cleared, I would park the "M "tractor and hop on the Ford tractor. The Ford had a bucket on the back, which was used to haul dirt from the barn yard to the cleared yard space. After I dumped the new dirt on the cleared space, I would prudently level and smooth it out. I would then stand back and admire my work, a smooth level stretch of dirt that I could envision as a lush lawn in the spring. I remember the pride I took in the transformation of our yard and even more than that, I was excited that Mom finally had a nice view when she looked out the kitchen window to the west.

By the end of the summer I had accomplished my goal. The entire cement slab had vanished and in its place was gorgeous black dirt that was smoothed out to be lawn the next year. I was elated and I knew it made Mom extremely happy. That endeavor laid the foundation for my thinking the rest of my life. To this day I never say, "can that be done?" but instead I question, "how can it be done"?

Chapter Forty-Five

TRACTOR TAXI

As we left Wood Lake School and walked towards home on the snow-packed gravel road, there was a change in the air. The week had been sort of a winter reprieve. We had experienced a snow filled winter but this week we had seen sunny skies and temperatures above zero most of the time. For me, the snow was a fun thing. It meant making snow forts, sledding down the creek bank by the outhouse and making snow angels all over the yard. For Dad it was not a good winter. Snow was already piled several feet high along the roads. The driveway into our farm was accessible only by this narrow, almost tunnel like path. I knew Dad was tired of moving the snow with the loader on the front of the "M" tractor, but for a six-year old boy, the winter had been perfect.

On our way home between jumping into the snow filled ditches and making paths along the road, we looked to the pale, gray western sky and knew change was coming. I was super excited when we arrived home. My brother Ronald was home for the weekend. He boarded in Lidgerwood because that is where he went to high school and for now there were no buses. It was always great when he was home. It seemed like Mom and Dad were happier and everybody had more fun. I looked up to Ronald in a way that only a brother who was eleven years younger could. Ronald would go sledding with us, he would play games with us and his stories about high school were fascinating. For certain, someday I would go to high school just like Ronald and I would be as smart as he.

We huddled under the feather tick blanket that night as the wind howled and the snow fell. Saturday was no different, more wind, more snow and the temperature dropped. As we played Monopoly in the living room, we could not even see out the windows as they were frost-covered from the cold. Sunday came in the same way. The snow had let up but the temperature was well below zero and the wind seemed like it was on a race track from western North Dakota to eastern Minnesota.

Mom told us that there would be no church, as the roads were blocked everywhere. That did not bother me as church was not that important to me at the age of six. Now, if it had meant missing Sunday School that would have been different. I had perfect attendance so far and that could not be compromised.

We had Mom's favorite Sunday dinner menu, fried egg sandwiches with a side of dill pickles. We even had mayo for our sandwiches. I think Dad tried to have things that Ronald liked, if he was going to be home. Suddenly it dawned on me. Ronald would not be able to get back to school because of the storm, so I would have him for at least another day of games and stories. I tried in vain to see out of the frost covered windows. Maybe, just maybe, this storm would last a long, long time.

Then Dad did the unthinkable. He got his winter parka on, put on his five buckle overshoes and ventured outside. I did not know why he would be doing that, as the snow was piled high, the driveway was blocked and I was sure nobody was going anyplace. I thought it was hard work just to get to the barn and feed the cows. It was mid-afternoon, in the middle of a *Touring* card game, when Dad returned to the house. He was carrying three medium rocks which he placed in the oven of the cook stove. I scratched my head and wondered what in the world he was doing. Then, like a bomb, he informed Ronald that they would be leaving in an hour! How that could happen was a mystery to me but it soon was revealed. Dad had gone into the shed and put the chains on the Ford tractor. He had attached a fifty-five gallon barrel onto the tractor hitch and then put fresh straw in the bottom. When the rocks were heated, they were placed in the barrel. The plan was to drive Ronald to Geneseo, where there was a main road to Lidgerwood. Dad would flag down someone and Ronald could ride to Lidgerwood so that he would not miss school on Monday. Of course my opinion did not count, but I thought it was a terrible idea. Why not have one more day of fun and games. School could not possibly be that important.

I think Dad was trying to get several points across. He wanted us to know how important school was, he wanted a challenge and adventure and maybe, he wanted to be a hero with a story to tell. Whatever his reason, he executed his plan to perfection and got Ronald to Lidgerwood. However, my memory is one of being denied more time and games with my brother.

Days after the taxi run

Chapter Forty-Six

NOT AGAIN DAD

Slides, that word could bring joy or boredom to the Lee family. It seemed there were two items that arose up in our family more often than any other things. If the day or the conversation was not about hunting, it was about photography.

Hunting; I never really got tired of hearing about that. Even I, when I was eight years old, could be part of that. I could not go deer hunting until I was older but pheasants I could. I should qualify my pheasant hunting days when I was young. I don't think I ever went pheasant hunting with Dad when I had a gun. When I was eight or nine, I served as the bird dog! *Carmen, go walk through those trees* or *Carmen walk over there through that brush.* In my adult life, I told more than one person that the reason I never took up pheasant hunting was because of my experience as a bird dog, it just was not that fun. I did not go duck hunting either. I guess Dad figured he did not need anyone to retrieve the ducks. But deer hunting was different. I went hunting deer many times. Even before I could go, I have wonderful memories of Dad, Dave and Ronald coming home from hunting with deer on top of the car. I also spent fun afternoons on the barn roof, waiting for them to arrive home.

This actually is not hunting, but shooting blackbirds was always a fun time. I could sit in my bedroom with the window screen off, and shoot them out of the big tree to the east of the house. I had to be careful that there weren't cars coming down the road beyond the trees. It was an easier shot if I could go north of the house towards the creek. There was a small grove of trees that almost hid the shop and gave welcome shade to the three-holer in the afternoon. I usually could get quite close and down a couple of birds before they flew away. I would then search the ground under the trees until I found the birds and take them to the legions of cats in the barn.

Sometimes, I would cross the fence by the trees, walk across the rock dam below our yard and meander over to the shelterbelt beyond the pasture. There, I could walk the entire length of trees and even see what was on Bert's land in the slough near our field. I could get shots at birds in one or both places most of the time. If I was lucky, I may even see a rabbit or fox on my way. Then and even today, I think about all the times Dad hunted and never provided a gun for me. My 22 I shot black birds with, was given to me by Ronald. He was in college and he came home with a gun and said it was mine. At that moment, he was about ten feet tall in my imagination. He told me it was a target rifle that he had modified just for me. Ronald said it should shoot really accurately and it did! Wow, I felt like I was the real deal and could hit anything I shot at.

Hunting was such a big deal for Dad, often it seemed to be bigger than life. It was for me, too, but my love of hunting was mixed with thoughts of no gun, or walking after fox in the winter with feet that felt frozen. Even larger than hunting in our lives was photography. I remember Dad sitting, night after night, in the winter reading his magazines and studying how to take better pictures. It was my routine to kiss Mom and Dad on both cheeks before I went to bed. It seemed to never fail, at that time Dad would be reading photography or hunting magazine. My bedtime routine of kissing both parents cheeks stopped when I got to high school but I doubt Dad's reading ever stopped. Was my bedtime routine a custom from Grandmas and Grandpas who came over from Norway? I never did ask.

When Dad wasn't reading, he was developing pictures. For many years it was in the kitchen with blankets covering the windows so no light came in. On nights he developed pictures, we kids were either in the living room playing games or upstairs getting ready for bed. We had to time things right because the kitchen door could only be opened at certain times. It was a great day when Dad finished his dark room, but that meant no more cook stove, so it really was a win-lose situation. It also meant that from that time on, Dad would often isolate himself in the dark room and we would not see him for hours.

Pictures entered our life in many ways. Dad always had his camera with him. It would not be unusual, in fact it may have been the norm, for him to see something along the road that he would stop and shoot with his camera. One time he was going to Lidgerwood and a very short time before he came to the tracks that crossed the road, the train derailed. Dad was johnny on the spot snapping pictures galore. For years, he would let people know that he was the first on the scene and he could prove it because he had pictures of the engine facing east. A short time after the derailment took place, they took the engine into Lidgerwood and came back with it so the engine was facing west! I also have a piece of rail in my garage today from the wreck!

Dad took family and wedding pictures as a way to earn money. Many Saturdays he and Mom were gone someplace for family or wedding pictures. I think Mom was the one who lined people up and put them in a good place for the pictures. I am guessing that Dad had thousands and thousands of prints he had developed. Sadly, they all went up in the fire when the farm burned. But the prints were not the items that often made my life boring and miserable. What I came to dislike in a big way were the slides that Dad took on all his trips.

He went on Farmers Union trips to New York City and Washington D C. I don't know what Washington D.C. and New York City had to do with Farmers Union, but that is where the trips took him. He would come home from those trips with hundreds of slides. Soon a pattern developed in our family. Dad would come home, pictures would arrive in about ten days and then company would come over to view the slides. Mom would invite people over for the evening. This usually took place in the winter because during the spring, summer and fall farmers were busy in the fields and there was daylight well into the evening. People would come over, there would be some conversation, which we children had to be part of, and then there was the dreaded question, "Would you like to see slides of my trip?" I don't remember anyone ever turning Dad down so we would sit through the pictures and narration one more time. We really had no choice but to watch. I am not sure why Dad insisted we watch time after time, but even if he would not have insisted the alternative was to go upstairs because the screen and slide projector were set up in the living room. The upstairs had no heat, so the only place to keep warm would have been in bed. Who wants to go to bed at 8:00 p.m. when there will be pie served at 9:00 p.m.?

So it was, picture, explanation, picture, explanation and on and on and on. I felt that it often bordered on bragging. It seemed like it took forever to get to the pie. I am sure by the tenth time or more I could have explained better and more concisely than Dad did and I think the company would have agreed. There was a tiny bit of relief when Dad would change the slide trays on the projector. That meant a brief intermission when we could make figures on the screen with our hands. I made a realistic looking rabbit; the best! The carrot at the end of a stick, the pie, really was not a just reward for the time spent sitting on the floor looking at Washington D. C. and New York City in the darkness of our living room. I still have the quiet voice in my mind pleading, "No Dad, not again".

March

Chapter Forty-Seven

MOTHER'S MARCH

Mom did many things for us kids. She performed everything from doctor, to teacher, to activity planner, baker and I would say at least a hundred other things. We were so grateful for many of the things she did and I am sure there were also many things we were not grateful for but should have been.

She often needed help in the garden and we were okay with that. We would be asked to do things like pick eggs, feed the cats, make sure the kerosene stove in the living room had fuel, mow the grass and other tasks that maybe we should have done without being asked. Sometimes she just did things on her own. I know there were many Sunday mornings when our shoes were lined up in the living room with a fresh coat of polish for church. It sounds kind of crazy but I think Mom liked to do that.

The most fun were the games she would let us play and the activities she would think up for us to spend our time on. One favorite activity was covering her drawings on the slate board with kernels of corn. Our slate board was a retired blackboard from school. It was slate, four feet by three feet and very heavy. Mom would draw a detailed picture on the slate and we would spend hours covering all the chalk marks with shiny yellow kernels of corn. That was usually done on rainy days. In the winter evenings we would often ask her if we could play ping pong on the kitchen table. We would have to ask because if Mom was baking or cooking in the kitchen we could not use the table for ping pong. She was often a big help in the puzzles we put together. Dave, Helen, Joan and I could be looking for a certain puzzle piece for a long time and then it was often Mom to the rescue.

Mom loved to play the piano. She could have sat at the piano for hours, if she had the time. She would usually play hymns from our church song book but there were times she would play old time or fun songs too. Dad would often sing solos in church and Mom would accompany him. That would often happen at Luther League which occurred on Sunday evening once a month in church. When we would hear Dad singing with Mom's playing in the evening after we had gone to bed we knew they would be singing and playing at the next Luther League gathering.

Mom's love of playing the piano came into play with one of our most fun activities. She would play this certain tune sometimes and it was perfect for marching. We liked it so much we would beg Mom to play it for us. She would only agree after we had begged her for some time. I think she enjoyed seeing and hearing how much we wanted her to play. Usually, after several appeals, she would sit at the piano and play the march. Before we started, we had to move all the chairs in the living room to the outside wall. We needed to make sure the kitchen chairs were out of the way and the big leaves for the kitchen table were not in. The table needed to be as small as possible. When Mom was satisfied all was in order, she would sit at the piano, make a big deal of sitting straight and make herself look like a professional pianist. It seemed like she always took too long, but finally she would start. We would begin in the living room, where the piano was, by lining up single file a few feet apart. Mom would put her fingers in place and the music would begin to softly fill the house. With her delicate fingers lightly touching the keys, we would slowly start out towards the kitchen with arms at our sides, feet lifting a little off the floor and our heads looking straight ahead. We would go around the kitchen table twice and then head back into the living room, doing a figure eight. As we finished the first round, Mom would look at us, smile and then her fingers would continue the march with more intensity and a little faster pace. We would finish our second round and there would be another nod, a bigger smile and the third round would begin. This time our arms would move back and forth, our feet would lift higher and we would throw our heads back a little.

We would continue to march round after round as long as Mom would play. By the time we got to round five or six, our arms were swinging as if they may come undone. Our feet would be stepping high in the air and our heads would be thrown back until our necks hurt. Finally Mom would stop. She would look at us as if she was worn out and could play no more. She knew what was coming next. "Mom, *play it again, please, just one more time!*" Sometimes she just had to quit because we had taken her from her work, other times we could convince her to play it again and again and again.

Marching never grew old and it did not know a season. We wanted to do it in the summer, in the winter and really anytime we could get Mom to play. We had so much fun marching to Mom's music, but really I am not sure who enjoyed it more, we kids or Mom!

Throughout my life, "Mom's March" comes to mind often. When it does, I hum it softly to myself and feel as if I am a much happier person for doing so.

Carmen, Dave, Ronald, John Mouw and Richard Aberle

Chapter Forty-Eight

DEER HUNTING

Hunting was imbedded into our lives on the farm. We would work hard but we would play hard too. Most of our days in the summer were work days. I do not think we worked to excess, but our mentality was you work each day and if you are lucky there may be some play time. When we were give play time, we thoroughly enjoyed ourselves.

Hunting took on three main objectives. One was to have fun, one was for sport and the other was to get food for the table. It was important to get the food, but really I know that Dad's focus was hunting the sport of hunting. It did not make any difference if the hunted was rabbits, gophers, ducks, geese, fox, deer or some other creature, the important thing was "the hunt".

I remember Dad coming home in the winter, after an all-day fox hunt. He would go into great detail of how they spotted the fox, the sport of out smarting it and then how, in the end, the fox ended up hanging on our granary wall where it would cure until Dad could take the pelt to Mr. Crandall for money. The fact that he hunted all day for one fox was not important. Later, as snowmobiles came into the sport, fox hunting changed, but Dad never participated in those hunts.

There were many winter trips to the Marble grove of trees several miles east of our farm. I never knew how it came to be called the Marble grove, but it certainly was a haven for cottontail rabbits. We would park the car along the road and walk the grove of trees, knee deep in snow. When we chased a cottontail rabbit up, there would be this loud noise from our 12 gauge shotguns and everyone would have a smile on their face, most of the time.

The plowed fields were home to many jack rabbits. We would cruise the roads, looking out into the furrows left by the plow. The rabbits would lie on the south side so we would drive on east/west roads. When we spotted a rabbit, we would stop and there would be this loud shot from the 243 gauge rifle. Sometimes, during Christmas vacation, we would spend days hunting rabbits. There is a terrifically sad story related to rabbit hunting, but that is not a story to be told now.

Gophers, were more plentiful than stars in the heavens. Uncle Obert's pasture and neighbor Bert's pasture, were both mainstays of gopher communities! With 22 rifles in hand, we would drive out into the pastures and shut the car off. There we could sit for hours. A soft whistle would usually entice the gophers to peep out of their hole and immediately there was one less gopher in that community!

Our farm land had plenty of sloughs, which provided a haven for ducks and geese. Really, the geese tended to come late in the fall and feed on the scattered corn or other grain. The ducks loved our farm sloughs. I sometimes wondered if "King Duck" paid dad to not drain our sloughs as so many farmers did at that time. I never grew fond of duck or goose meat but the hunting was grand.

The hunting of these animals paled to the comparison of deer hunting. Deer were the prize. We had deer around our farm but we seldom hunted near home. It just was not very fun to jump in the car and go out early in the morning looking for deer. It may have been more practical, more cost effective and equally as successful as going out west, but in no way would it have been as much fun. Deer hunting meant travel, it meant camaraderie and it was full of tradition. It seemed like we never had money but when it came to deer hunting we had knives, rifles, ammunition and the means to travel to western North Dakota for the hunt.

There were two different venues I remember when hunting. The first was hunting on Sam Wheeler's ranch. We did that two or three years while I was in high school. Sam had a ranch and was struggling to stay afloat. The first year we hunted with him, his house was old and downtrodden. We slept in the loft with little bedding. The second year we arrived, he was in a new house with fancy furniture and many bedrooms. Oil had been discovered on his land and the oil checks paid for everything. Each year we hunted with Sam, we filled our deer tags.

Soon after the oil boom, Sam sold his ranch and moved to Wyoming. For the next several years we traveled to the badlands in North Dakota and camped in John Mouw's camper. That was perhaps the utopia of my hunting days.

The hunting experience would start on Monday or Tuesday. Mom would bake fresh buns while Dad would go to Lidgerwood to buy salami, cheese, candy bars and apples. Dad would tell me what rifle I would be using and I would clean it, shine it and put it in the case. I would then get my hunting knife out. It would be cleaned, oiled and sharpened. On Thursday, after school, we would head west towards our hunting destination. We would arrive in the Badlands late Thursday evening and set up camp. Deer hunting opened Friday noon. Most of the time, we would have one or two deer by Friday evening. Saturday morning Dad would get up in the dark and by the time I woke up, the aroma of eggs and deer liver would fill the camper. We would eat breakfast, pack a lunch off we would go with a place in mind to meet at lunch time. The Badlands were so beautiful that I expected to see a deer each time I came over a hill. Of course that did not happen, but it made for wonderful days.

Deer hunting provided much of our meat for the year. We had cattle, but they were sold to provide money for farm expenses. There were years when we would harvest 3, 4 or 5 deer. The butchering and packaging of the deer was always an exciting time for me. I loved helping Dad cut up the deer and grind the meat into deer burgers.

Deer hunting not only provided food but it supplied lifelong lessons in anatomy, knife sharping and different cuts of meat.

I am not sure when I was old enough to hunt deer but I think it was about age fourteen. Before that time, when I was too young to go, I would shimmy up the light pole by the barn and lie on the west roof looking for Dad and Dave to come home. When I was sure the dust in the distance was them, I would scamper down the pole and run to the house to tell Mom. I would then wait in the yard until the car pulled up to the front door. The anticipation of what deer they bagged always caused my heart to race. I always hoped they would bring home a huge deer with antlers three feet across! Often, there would be at least one large deer but antlers three feet across, that never happened.

The day that I could go, and not watch for them to come home, was kind of like passing from childhood to manhood. It made me feel like I was an adult and from that time on I considered myself to be a man among men.

Dad, Dave, Ronald and Carmen after a successful pheasant hunt
Notice the wind charger on the house, it gave us daily electricity
for one light bulb and maybe the radio for a few hours before
rural electricity (REA) came to the farm in the 50's

206

Carmen on the best wheels ever, his
Harley Davidson 250 Sprint

Chapter Forty-Nine

WHEELS

Growing up I did not have the best wheels and by wheels, I mean transportation. As a child, wheels consisted of a bike and later in college it meant a motorcycle.

My very first wheels were the little bike on the farm. Of course one cannot travel too far on a little red Schwinn bike with tattered red and white seat, shiny fenders and 24 inch tires, but it was a grand way to travel. It took me the half mile to the lake, out to the mail box after Fritz came with the mail, down to the bridge to look for turtles and actually any place a six year old boy wanted to go. I learned how to repair a flat, clean and oil the greasy chain, polish the chrome fenders and bend the handle bars back after crashing on gravel roads. After my brother Dave left for college, I graduated from the little bike to the big bike and that too got me anyplace I was allowed to venture and I felt it gave me more freedom. That also was a one-speed bike with a back pedal brake, but it had bigger rims and bigger tires so I could go faster and farther than ever. I could go as far as Grandmas' house to get her delicious, mouthwatering cookies. My all-time favorite was the chewy oatmeal with big dark lumps of chocolate melted inside. I was pretty successful in avoiding her cookies with raisins.

My first real driving took place on our little Ford tractor. It was gray with red trim, wide front wheels and a hidden gas tank right in front of the steering wheel. We had a mower, a plow, a disc and a scoop for the back of it. Each of them attached to the hydraulic hitch which went up and down with the easy movement of a long lever on the right side. I could drive it at the tender age of six because the clutch was a push down type which was easy to use. I am not sure the Ford tractor would be classified as wheels in the sense of getting places, but maybe so. I started driving it the same summer that I learned to ride the little bike. I considered myself one of the men on the farm then and was sure farming was a fun way of life until Dad sent me out to help pick rocks because I could now drive! The International "M" tractor was different. It had tall rear tires and two smaller tires on a narrow front end. You had to be kind of manly and strong to push the clutch in so I could not drive that until I became a teenager. Well, maybe not that old but I couldn't drive it until I was strong enough to push the clutch in.

"Big Red," our wonderful truck, was a different story. It had a flathead-8 engine with a muffler that was quick to rust out so the sound when one drove it was next to heaven for a young man. It was big, it was old and it had the manual transmission that you had to double clutch. By that I mean you pushed the clutch in to take it out of the gear, release the clutch and then push it in again to put it into the higher gear. The gear shifting lever was this long handle on the floor. I really cannot remember when I was allowed to drive that but it was a manly task for sure. To be old enough and smart enough and tall enough to see through the crank out window and to double clutch and then to steer was a task only for the brave and not for the faint of heart, so I believed. Actually I am not sure you would call the truck "wheels" either as it was mostly driving to, from and in the fields. Dave and I did take it to a Farmer's Union meeting one time Mom and Dad were gone. We found out the next day that we were told to walk because Big Red had no water in the radiator! That is another story for sure. Big Red may not even be classified as a truck by today's standards but back in the 50's with its muscle, its sound, its hydraulic hoist and its crank out front window, it was in a class of its own.

For sure, the true wheels of my young life was the one car we had on the farm as I grew up. It was a 1953 Ford with a flat 8 engine, no power steering, vacuum windshield wipers[1], a bench front seat and good looking hub caps with "Ford" on them. It was two-tone green with scrapes and rust but most of the time all was covered up by dirt and grime from the gravel roads. I think flat 8 engines were the standard back then. I remember Dad making fun of a neighbor, when he bought a six cylinder car. Heaven help, what Dad thought when four cylinder engines became the rage! Dad was trained as a mechanic and he could fix anything on the car. The problem was it seemed that the car really wanted to fall apart and enter Ford heaven at the next turn. I had NO confidence in the car. I think it only really failed me once, but in my mind it was always on the brink of disaster! As I packed my suitcase to leave for college in the fall of 1965, I really said good-bye to the farm and to the car.

For a short time Dad had this pickup. It actually would have been a nice pick up a generation earlier. I drove it the summer after my senior year of high school. Here the year is nineteen sixty-five and I am cranking my wheels to start! Well, I have to say it was so off the charts that maybe, just maybe, it was "in". The next spring Art, the gas man, came out to deliver gas and offered Dad a hundred dollars for the pickup. For a hundred dollars Dad sold my brother Dave's dream of restoration, too.

My next set of wheels was a trusty single-speed Schwinn bike that I purchased for fifteen dollars or so in the fall of my freshman year of college. Those wheels got me any place I wanted to go. I was good to go that year for wheels, but a blip on the radar came up in the spring. My mother asked if I could come home for the summer. That was the last thing I wanted to do. Here I was, on my own and away from our antique farm that my folks seemed to enjoy so much. I had visions of no more harvest dust from the thistles, no more rock picking and no more lonely Sunday afternoons golfing on my personal homemade golf course with Player, Nicklaus and Palmer. Palmer always won as he was so much better than Nicklaus. Well, I just could not admit that Palmer was aging and Nicklaus was coming in to be the star of the PGA Tour. Anyway, I told my mom that I could not come home without wheels. My bike would not do it on the farm and Dad had sold the pickup. She came up with the idea that Dad said he would be willing to help me purchase a motorcycle and would give me five hundred dollars for working. That got my attention in a hurry. I would have a motorcycle, no expenses and some money for the fall. I could live with that as board, room and school tuition had cost me $1200 my freshman year in college. I knew, in the fall, my work study job would pay me a dollar an hour and I could work up to twenty-five hours a week. Done deal, I would go home for the summer.

On a cold blustery Saturday in late April Dad and I drove to Aberdeen, South Dakota. I had to decide between a 1964 red Harley Davidson Sprint for $400 and a 1965 black Harley Davidson Sprint for $500. As I drove home on my shiny black 250 Harley, little did I know that I was embarking on a new "wheels" adventure. It turned out to be my all-time favorite wheels! My friend, Larry, had a 350 Honda Scrambler and we traveled everywhere the following year. There were times I would put on my shiny brown Bostonian slip on shoes, my charcoal pleated cuffed pants, my baby blue mock turtle neck shirt under my navy blazer and I thought I could pretty much fetch any young gal I desired. Well, I didn't really try but then young men dream dreams! I did think I was kind of a dashing young man though. I had my Sprint all of my sophomore year of college but kept it in the basement of our apartment in the cold winter months. My winter transportation consisted again of my trusty Schwinn bike with almost flat tires.

Wheels, they come and they go. They take you places you want to go, places you need to go and places maybe you should not go! They can be pedal powered or gas powered but whatever the choice, they do contribute to memories that last a lifetime.

Chapter Fifty

MY FISH CORRAL

When I was growing up I loved to catch fish but I did not like to eat them. I really disliked Mom's fish dinners because all we had were perch and northern pike. When Mom took them out of the fry pan and put them on the table they looked like dead soldiers with swords sticking out in all directions. I never asked but apparently Dad did not know how to filet fish. He just cleaned them, took the scales off the northern pike and they were then ready for the fry pan in Mom's kitchen. The taste was okay but by the time my mouth had explored all avenues of the fish, searching for those swords, it was like a piece of cold milk toast going down my throat. I made matters worse because when I eat, I like to take a bite of each thing in a big mouthful but the corn and potatoes did not mix well with the bony fish. At times I needed to spit out my food to get the bones and when I did it looked like a matzo ball with spikes!

I did not enjoy eating fish but fishing was one of my favorite things to occupy my time. The best was when I could walk or ride my bike to Lake Tewaukon. During my childhood days I came to believe Lake Tewaukon belonged to me. Fishing alone at my lake was much more fun than going with Dad. He seemed to believe fish only were hungry early in the morning. When I went fishing with Dad, we would get up, eat breakfast, make some sandwiches and be out the door before the sun woke up!. My favorite fishing time was when Dad went on an all-day errand and failed to tell me what work to do. On those rare days, I would inform mom that I was going fishing and then for the next several hours I would be in my own little world, without a care or concern in the world.

The first thing I had to do was get bait. That meant getting our old rusty shovel from the dilapidated shed. Usually I could find it standing against the wall next to the window with broken glass. I figured it got rusty because rain would come in that window and settle on the shovel blade. Each time I got the shovel, I would ask myself why Dad never fixed it or for that matter the other broken things on the farm that needed attention. I later realized that dad was not a farmer; he was a hunter and photographer. He lived on a farm and put in crops because he needed the money to support himself and his family but a farmer he was not. With shovel in hand I would head to the grove of trees north of the house and behind our three holer near the cow pasture. I had found, through trial and error, that worms loved the warm moist soil where the grass met the shrubs on the tree line very near the outhouse. I kept an old Folgers coffee can just for my worms. I always carefully placed it in the far corner of the shed where I knew nobody would find it. Really nobody wanted an old can but there was always an outside chance that my brother, my sister or even Mom would spot it and throw it away. On my fishing days, I would carefully pick my way over the boards, onto the rusty plow and there, snug in the corner, was my Folgers coffee can. With can and shovel in hand, it was a short order to dig, put some moist dirt in the can, separate those plump, squishy worms from the dirt the shovel turned over and place them in the can. I always placed a nice clump of moist dirt on top. It seemed to me that the worms actually liked it there. Perhaps they felt secure in that confined place.

With worms in hand, I retrieved my old but shiny Shakespeare reel from the corner of the barn. I kept my reel in the barn because I knew it would stay dry and rust free. Next retrieval was my tackle box which was hidden in the hay barn, nice and dry and out of sight of my siblings. In my tackle box, which was dull green with a large dent in the top, I had hooks, bobbers that I called corks, extra line and red and white Dare Devils. The Dare Devils were for northern pike but when I went fishing by myself I would only fish for perch. The Folgers can, the tackle box and the rod and reel were more than a load for my bike so usually I would walk. Sometimes I would manage to carry all those things and ride the bike but it was difficult and I think I looked like a circus act about to fail. I could bike from the front door to the lake without touching the handlebars but carrying things made balancing a bit tricky so I tended to not do that. After saying good-bye to Mom, I headed to my lake with gear in hand. My journey took me past the outhouse, a jump over the pasture fence, across the rock dam below our house, another jump over the pasture fence again and then I was at neighbor Bert's pasture. It was easy to walk through his pasture, as he always over-grazed his cows so his pasture consisted of rocks, gopher holes and grass chewed down to the very roots.

One summer I made a three-hole golf course in Bert's pasture. I could use gopher holes for the cups as long as I put a piece of wood in the hole preventing the ball from going down to the gopher's living room! The trouble with the pasture golf course was cows tended to mess up the fairways big time. As I left his pasture I always walked right through Bert's front yard because his farm bordered the lake. Once in a while I would get lucky and Bert's wife, Eleanor, would see me walking in the yard and would offer me a cookie. I actually hoped she would because I loved cookies, especially her peanut butter cookies.

When I arrived at the lake, it was a short climb down to the water. I had a path well-worn so it was the same way each time. The only obstacle was a large rock in the middle of the path. I would make a game of it and pretend I was a rock climber up in the mountains. Each time I would find a different way to conquer my difficult decent. My favorite way was to place my fishing things on the side of the rock as low as I could reach, turn over on my belly and slide down the rock until my toes, I usually was barefoot, touched the dirt below and then I would pretend I was making a great move by getting over that huge boulder. As I lowered myself off that huge boulder I would reach up, get all my gear and there I stood at the water's edge of my lake.

My first order of business was to make a corral. I had no intention of eating my fish. Why would I go to the trouble of cleaning them and then taking half an hour to pick out the bones? I would catch them, put them in my personal corral and keep them there until the sun was low in the sky and I knew it was time to go home and milk the cows. At that time, I would carefully take one of the small stones out and watch the perch swim away to be caught another day. I would always dismantle the entire corral as it had to be different each time. After I fashioned my corral, it was time to search for the longest, plumpest worm and squeeze it onto the hook. Then I would fasten the cork on the line about a foot above the hook and throw it into the water. With a mighty heave, the cork would be launched into my lake. In mid-summer the sun was high enough so that as I sat on the rocky edge of the lake I could sit back in warm sunshine and enjoy my private fishing lake. I would often pretend that I was fishing in the ocean way off shore. During these times I had no troubles, no cares and the world seemed to be at my fingertips.

As the sun lazily settled low in the sky, it was time to get home and milk the cows. I would usually have about a dozen fish in my corral by then. It was funny because even though the corral was about two feet by two feet, it could hold huge fish. One time as the bobber went down and I pulled the line, I had a large whale that took an hour to land. Another time it was a shark that fought to the bitter end. It seemed that each time I went fishing, it was a different size and a different fish but I was always the great fisherman who would conquer all. When I arrived home, I would tell Mom how great I was and she would agree with me that I was special. My reel never failed me, my line never tangled and I caught my limit each time. Perhaps the best part was I always let the fish go to be caught another day by the great fisherman.

Our rural school years after it closed

Chapter Fifty-One

WOOD LAKE SCHOOL

One-room rural schools frequented the landscape in North Dakota during the first half of the twentieth century. They were built so that farm families would not have to travel far for the children to attend school. There were three rural schools within a six mile radius of our farm. We were a mile and a half from Wood Lake School. Dad and Mom attended Wood Lake, as well as I and my four older siblings. By the time Helen, the youngest started school, we were being bused to Cayuga Elementary School.

In the fifties, the rural schools started to close and buses roamed the country roads picking up children and transporting them to town. In the spring of 1956, the doors of Wood Lake School were closed. The building became a gathering place for the farming community, a voting place in November and it continued to be a place for Farmers' Union meetings. No more classes and no more children walking the gravel roads to and from school. The building remains there to this day, but in a dilapidated state. With bare walls and floors, broken windows and a deserted look it seems to be going the way of V-8 cars and film cameras, obsolete and unwanted!

In its day, Wood Lake had much charm. When you drove into the school yard there, in front of you, was a square, white building with a bell tower on the entrance. As you entered the building you were in a cloak room with a high ceiling and two rows of coat hooks, one low and one high. To the right was the door to the lunch room. That was where we served goodies at Farmers Union meetings and during school we served commodities, from the government, which supplemented the cold lunches we brought from home. The best government commodity was canned peaches, I thought they were delicious. The first thing you saw when you left the cloak room and entered the classroom was a pot-belly stove, which was our sole source of heat in the winter. The north wall was a place to hang pictures and papers while the east was all slate board. That may have been one of the places I had to write my name a hundred times, as punishment for talking too much! The entire south wall consisted of many windows and the west wall was more slate board with the teacher's desk in front of it. The outside of the building was a typical school yard, except for the two out-houses, one for the girls and one for the boys. There was a huge slide, high swings, a large merry-go-round and two teeter-totters. Near the swings was the water pump where, which we drank from and got our water for the cooler in the school. In the front of the school was a large flag pole where we raised and lowered the flag each day. After we raised the flag in the morning, we would go inside and all stand with our hands over our heart as we repeated the pledge of allegiance to the flag. There was an open space between the school and the road on the north where we could play ball. Home base was near the boys' out-house and if you hit the ball over the road on the west side of school, it was a home run.

We walked to school most of the time. With cheese sandwiches, made from commodity cheese, and saltine crackers in our lunch buckets, we walked the mile and a half which gave us enough time to kick stones on the gravel road and throw stones at fence posts in Uncle Obert's pasture. During our walk we also discussed if there would be a way we could get the teacher to give us an extra recess that day. Our school day ended at 3:30 and we would sometimes hurry home so we could listen to *The Lone Ranger* and then *Sargent Preston and Yukon King* on the radio. We did not have a television. Sometimes Dad or Mom would drive us to and from school if it was really cold. I enjoyed walking in the snow and jumping in the snow filled ditches, but if I saw our car coming I knew our fun filled frosty walk was over. If I suspected Mom was coming, I would be sure to pull my earlaps down. She would almost have a fit if she saw my ears sticking out of my cap. I am not sure why, but she gave me the idea that my ears were too big!

I remember sometimes we had the same workbook as the year before. It seemed to me that most of our rural education was memorizing things. By the time I was in third grade I could remember the spelling of the words from the year before. Sound out a word, what does that mean? Math consisted of memorizing the facts tables. When I entered Cayuga School in the fourth grade, one of the first things we did in math was our facts tables. We would get a paper with 100 problem such as 2x1=__, 2x2=__, 2x3=__ etc. I remember I finished mine and most of the students were not even half done. If you do your facts tables for three years you should pretty much have them down! My memorization skills made me look like I was really smart when in reality many of my classmates were "academically challenged"!

At Wood Lake our winter time recesses would consist of games in the room or bundling up and going outside to play in the snow. We built forts, had snowball fights and made snow angels all over the yard. In our snowball fights, the best place to hide was behind the boys' out-house. We would also make a big ring in the snow, wearing our five buckle overshoes, and make paths in and out of it. The game was then duck, duck, gray duck. In the spring it was playing in the snow filled ditches and then in the water as the spring melt occurred. More than once I had to take my clothes off, put my coat on and dry my clothes on the pot-belly stove. The teacher did allow me to change in the cloak room. She was not happy when several students came in all wet! I know I came in wet more than anyone.

My last year, grade three; we had twelve students in the eight grades. I had one classmate, Dwayne. Dave and Joan were also in school that year and I think they both had classmates too. It probably did not make a lot of difference, as often two or three grades would have the same books. I know I had the same spelling book in grades one, two and three.

Discipline was usually done in one of two ways. The teacher would write a sentence on the board and then tell the student to write it 500 times or a 1000 times. Another way was to tell the student they had to fill two or three or four pages, on both sides, with their first, middle and last name. I am sure that is why I have awful handwriting. I must have talked a lot, because I remember writing and writing and writing. It came to the point that I would write my name on many pages and keep the paper in my desk. When I was told to write my name 1000 times I would draw horses for a while and then take the papers, with my name written on them, out of my desk and hand them in. I did get caught one time as the teacher thought it did not take me enough time to get the writing finished. Thinking back on those days in Wood Lake, I think I was bored a lot. Regardless, that is my rationale for having to write my name so often!

It would be easy to think that our rural education was mostly a waste of time but when I look at students who came out of Wood Lake, they usually did well in college and in life. Educators, pilots, farmers, businessmen and many other professions emerged from the rural schools in North Dakota so I think there was much good going on, even if it was difficult to see at the time.

I found out, in the fall of 1956, how fun Wood Lake School was. In September of that year, I got on the bus at 7:10 AM and arrived in Cayuga about 8:30. It did not take me long to realize that walking the dusty gravel roads to Wood Lake was way more fun than riding the bus for a long time. Later, in high school, the ride became a two hour ride. The trade-off was in my classmates. Instead of one classmate I had twenty-four, and that was much more fun. There were more ball games, more things happening in the classroom and a lot of books to read. Also, there was hot lunch every day which I enjoyed.

For most of us, the one-room rural schools are a distant memory. The reading, the writing, the memorization and of course the recesses, dance around in our memories and we smile as we sip our morning coffees. Were those good times? I would say they were wonderful. All of life has its ups and downs and for sure Wood Lake had them too. If I could go back and trade those times for something different, there is no way I would agree to that.

Bergen Church

Chapter Fifty-Two

A DEFINING MOMENT

I have had a few defining moments in my life. Some have been relatively minor yet have changed the path of my life. Some have been catastrophic and left me wallowing for a long time. This is a story of a simple "dare" that had a huge influence in my life.

Growing up, my family attended a small rural Lutheran Church, Bergen. It was nestled in the midst of farm country in southeastern North Dakota. There was another Lutheran church a scant two miles away, Palestine. During my childhood, I could not figure out why there were two churches so close. As an adult, I asked my mom and she told me that Palestine was primarily Swedish and Bergen was primarily Norwegian.

Bergen Church was very much a part of my childhood. We had church every other Sunday, as that was the only time our pastor was available. Actually, Sunday School was more important than church for me. Right behind Sunday School was Luther League and other church functions like the fall bazaar. During the fall bazaar, we could buy ice cream cones for a nickel, gum for a nickel and other goodies. I would work in the fall at home carrying corn cobs into the house as every few buckets Dad or Mom would give me a nickel! Sunday school was an important time for me. I am not sure if the content was as important as the quizzes between the boys and girls or if the "perfect attendance" was the main draw. Actually I do know, it was "perfect attendance" that was the most important thing to me, but the quizzes were close behind. I guess that means the content came in third place!

Luther League was a monthly event. It was designed to be run by the young people. We met in the church sanctuary. For the meeting, adults sat near the back and all the high school students sat near the front. Most of the time, the women would be in the basement getting goodies ready for the most important part of Luther League. The meeting was actually just a formality as there was seldom, if ever, any old or new business. The focus was supposed to be on the program, but really for the kids, our main focus was the goodies. There would be hymns sung by everyone, maybe a solo by Dad, maybe a reading by one of the kids and then it was time for refreshments. Everyone would gather in the basement for cake, cookies, Kool-Aide and coffee. I would say Luther League was five minutes of meeting, twenty minutes of program and forty-five minutes of goodies.

Given what Luther League was, it is strange that it was the setting of a major defining moment in my life. I was the Luther League president when I was a sophomore. It meant I had to conduct the meeting which was not a big deal. The one boy I related to at Luther League was Chuckie. He went to Lidgerwood High School so the only time I saw him was at church functions. Chuckie, some girls and I were talking one Luther League night over Kool-Aide and cookies. I had been reading this book; The Power of Prayer by Norman Vincent Peale, and I was into it in a serious way. I was sharing how powerful prayer was and how we should be spending more time with the Lord. I thought that we could do great things if we would pray more. Chuckie looked at me, with a hint of his silly grin, and said, "You should give a speech about it at Luther League next month". Without blinking an eye and certainly without discerning if he was serious I replied, "That is a great idea"! As soon as the words came out of my mouth, I questioned my sanity. Did I really say that? Did I really mean that? I was not one to back down so I began to think about the Luther League meeting in August.

For the next month, that was pretty much all I thought about. I had never spoken in front of a crowd of adults and fellow students. I believed I was beyond my stuttering stage, but I wasn't sure about that in front of a crowd. Each night, as I went to bed, I would read and reread parts of the book. Then as I was falling asleep I would go over and over aloud, what I would say. I never wrote anything down. I just repeated and repeated what I felt I wanted to get across. I was afraid of what I had gotten myself into but yet I was so convinced about "prayer" that I went forward each day repeating my talk.

It was during harvest and the week before the meeting Dad and I were the only ones in the harvest field. Dad would drive the combine for the first three tanks of wheat. The truck would then be full and I would drive the combine while he took the load to Geneseo. Usually, I would have the combine tank full well before he returned from town. When the tank was full I would stop and wait for Dad. While I waited, I would practice my speech. I took a hand full of wheat kernels and put them on the tractor seat. The seat had many holes in it. I would then stand on the seat and as I maneuvered the seeds through the tractor seat holes with my big toe, I would recite my speech out loud. I had the speech down so I could finish it about the time all the seeds were through the holes. When Dad returned, I would then sit in the truck and repeat it to myself time after time after time. No notes, just memory.

Finally, Luther League night arrived on the last Sunday in August. We drove to Bergen and I was a mess. I was afraid of stuttering, my hands were clammy, my armpits were damp and my head was spinning. What would I do if I stood up in front of everyone and could not utter a word? Mom knew what I was going to do and she assured me that I would do fine but in my mind I felt I was in for a failure. It helped when I thought back to Chuckie's "dare" because I knew I couldn't live with myself if I failed. I opened the meeting on time and prayed that there would be old or new business, but nothing but nothing happened to delay the inevitable. I thought, couldn't they discuss something? But of course I knew that was not going to happen. I may have even said something like, "Lord, what about one of your miracles?" I then sat down and Chuckie, who was vice president, stood up and announced that Carmen would give a talk. As I rose to my feet, my legs shook, my knees wobbled and I could feel perspiration running down my back. I started to talk but I did not know who was speaking. My voice, which at the age of 15 was a man's voice, seemed to be high pitched and crackly. Slowly I gathered my wits and proceeded to give the message I wanted. As I came to the closing, I glanced towards the back and there stood several women who were supposed to be fixing goodies in the basement. Why were they listening to me? One woman had tears and I thought I must have said something wrong. I finished my speech with a verse from the bible; *"If God is with you, who can be against you? Pray and God will listen."* When it was finally over, I sat down with a sigh of relief but also with a resolve that I had said what I believed in. I was embarrassed as my shirt was soaked and tiny beads of sweat were etching lines down my cheeks. But, I was finished and I had not failed.

Driving home, Dad was silent but Mom said she was proud of me. She said that one of the women was touched to the point of tears. I was relieved that I had not said something wrong. I sat up straight when Mom mentioned that someone thought I should be a pastor when I grew up. I have had peaks and valleys in my life but prayer has always been a big part, regardless of what I have done. That hot August night in Bergen Church was a defining moment.

FARM--CAN I CHANGE?

The wind
It came from afar
Often it blew storms of
Rain, hail and snow

The sun
It was a beacon
Of soft warm light at times
Of stifling heat at times

One could look west
The distant horizon
It seemed to invite
the land and sky to meet as friends

As I walked
Into the grassy fields
The plants and weeds good and bad
They seemed to nod in passing

On wind swept fields stones stared
Into chiseled and weathered faces
Creatures big and small
Scurried from place to place

The lazy peaceful creek
It meandered
From south to north
Welcoming and saying good-bye

In this land was
Life to celebrate
Death to mourn
Memories to cherish

The bent and stunted trees
They seemed to beg
More rain for me
Less wind for me

The washboard roads
They wore a constant coat
Of gravely dust from the earth
It seemed so shabby

The grassy ditches
They followed the roads
Like a good friend
Giving character to them

One could gaze afar
Out on the fertile fields
Where golden grain waved
As if to greet you hello

The rich dark soil
It seemed to know
It had a purpose
To give of itself

There in the middle
Of this desolate country
Stood an old rustic farm
Majestic yet sunken

It wanted to burst
Into a new song
A new beginning
Just for a time

Could it not go
Back to a time
When all was well
When it stood tall

It seemed to know
It was not to be
It had its place
It must be content

Why this dilapidated farm
Of old antiques
Could it not change
Just for a short while

Why must it remain
As an old man
Content to live
In the memories of the past

After all it was home
To a family
A family that remained
Married to the past--content

Then one hot dry spring day
A blustery wind caught a fiery spark
The farm was no more
All evaporated into smoke and ashes

Carmen James Lee
January 24, 2013

225

Epilogue

I attended rural Wood Lake School for three years, Cayuga Elementary for five years and graduated from Sargent Central High School in Forman, North Dakota. North Dakota State University, Minot College and University of North Dakota were among several insitutions of higher learning I attended. I obtained my MA in Education in 1976.

There were six children in our family. The oldest, Lawrence (Ronald or Red) was born in 1936 and Helen, born in 1950, was number six. A history of my siblings:

Ronald married Glorine and they had one child, Roxanne. Glorine married, sometime after Ronald's sudden and unexpected death in 1964, Charlie who was a pastor, writer and cowboy. Daughter, Roxanne, died unexpectedly in 2013. Charlie preceded Roxanne in death in 2004.

Janet married John Mouw and their two children were Robert and Esther. In the winter of 1966, Janet suddenly became ill and died within a couple of days. John remarried and he and Judi have one child, Becky.

Joan married Ronald (Ron) Sandness. Their children are Brian and Quinn. The story for them is they have six great grandchildren, four of which are quadruplets! Joan and Ron celebrated their 50th anniversary in 2011. They reside in Sandy, Utah.

Dave married Marlys and they have two children, Lisa and Coleen. Dave and Marlys will celebrate their 50th anniversary in 2015. They reside in Jamestown, North Dakota.

Helen married Michael Petteway. Michael brought two daughters into their marriage so Helen gets to spoil a grandson and a granddaughter! Michael died in 2013. Helen currently resides in Holiday Island, Arkansas.

What kind of careers do rural children take up? Ronald was in education, Janet was in education and a homemaker, Joan was in retail, Dave was in education and Helen was in business. I would say that is not bad for children who grew up on mush (milk and flour), wheat berries, venison, eggs, choke cherry syrup and brought cheese and egg sandwiches for lunch during the time they attended the one room rural school. We experienced much tragedy in deaths and the burning of our farm, but country folks are resilient.

I married Gail Saunders in 1968, after my junior year in college. After graduation we lived in Devils Lake, North Dakota, for several years before moving to St. Paul, Minnesota. Our marriage brought four children into our lives; John, married to Mary, Travis, single, Aaron, married to Amy and Cynthia, married to Michael. John is in education, Travis has been in business, Aaron is in retail and Cynthia, a teacher and a homemaker. Spouses include Mary, a teacher who is currently a homemaker, Amy is in business and Michael is in education. Along with in-laws, came grandchildren; Henry, Liam, Leo, Faustina, Audrey, Jude, Ruby, Benedict, Agatha, Elspeth and Veronica.

I retired, in 2007, after spending thirty-eight years as an administrator and teacher in education of the deaf and hard of hearing. Since retiring I have spent time traveling, doing woodworking and writing, among other things.

Gail died in 2009, after battling breast cancer for several years. In 2011, I married Terry, who was a friend and classmate from high school. We reside in Naples, Florida but spend summers in our home in St. Paul, Minnesota. We purchased a teardrop camper in 2012 and have made it our mission to visit all the national parks. By the winter of 2014-2015 we have visited fifty-one of the fifty-nine national parks while traveling over 35,000 miles. Our travels have taken us as far north as Coldfoot, Alaska, as far west as Ventura, California, as far south as Key West and to the east coast.

How did I come to write this book? I started blogging in 2009 and realized that I loved to write. Many people said they enjoyed reading my blog. When grandchildren visited they would beg to hear "Grandpa's stories". In the fall of 2012 Terry read an article about writing a 50,000 word book in a month. Knowing I was not interested in fiction, she challenged me to write childhood stories each day during November. I took on the challenge but extended it through December. Thirty months later, not one month, my book is a reality. So, blogging, storytelling and a challenge resulted in this book venture. Even though writing a book has been an arduous task, I have so thoroughly enjoyed telling my tales that there may be glimmers of a second book in the works. I did say maybe!

I take full responsibility for the content of this book. Terry edited it but with my style and choice of words her task was difficult at best. If you see errors, they are mine. If my siblings remember some of the details differently you may be right but I tried my best. My goal was to give my children and grandchildren memories of my childhood. To that end I say, "Enjoy".

65302879R00147

Made in the USA
Lexington, KY
08 July 2017